the
leader's
brain

Michael L. Platt

the leader's brain

**ENHANCE YOUR LEADERSHIP,
BUILD STRONGER TEAMS,
MAKE BETTER DECISIONS, AND
INSPIRE GREATER INNOVATION
WITH NEUROSCIENCE**

WHARTON
SCHOOL
PRESS
Philadelphia

Published by Wharton School Press
The Wharton School
University of Pennsylvania
3620 Locust Walk
300 Steinberg Hall-Dietrich Hall
Philadelphia, PA 19104
Email: whartonschoolpress@wharton.upenn.edu
Website: wsp.wharton.upenn.edu

Ebook ISBN: 978-1-61363-098-3
Paperback ISBN: 978-1-61363-099-0

Contents

Introduction

When Hurricane Maria, a deadly Category 4 storm, ravaged Puerto Rico in 2017, news coverage focused on the catastrophic human toll. More than 3,000 people lost their lives, and the 3 million who survived dealt with physical devastation of their communities, job loss, lack of clean water and food, and the worst blackout in US history.

But Maria also ravaged another population. I have been studying the inhabitants of Cayo Santiago, also known as Monkey Island, for the past 13 years. The island is home to about 1,700 rhesus macaque monkeys, and it also took a direct hit from the hurricane. The devastation included severe flooding and damage to most of the vegetation. All the infrastructure was destroyed, including the rainwater-collecting cisterns that provided fresh water and the feeding corrals where researchers provisioned food that supplemented what the monkeys foraged from the island.

Since the hurricane, my team here at Wharton and the University of Pennsylvania School of Medicine, as well as our many collaborators at other institutions, have been studying the impact of both immediate and lingering stress on the brain and on the body. We're learning not just what stress does to us but how we can fight its effects. The monkeys—all of which survived the storm but exhibit classic signs of exposure to stress—are showing us how we can better protect ourselves. The insights we're gaining could help leaders decide how to invest in solutions that support their teams and employees and, in the process, reduce the estimated $300 billion that US companies currently spend on the health costs, absenteeism, and poor performance that result from workplace stress.

The author is pictured with rhesus macaque monkeys on the island of Cayo Santiago.

Perhaps the most important lesson the Cayo monkeys have taught us is that social support is critical to successfully navigating disasters. In the aftermath of Hurricane Maria, monkeys not only became more tolerant of each other but actively reached out and made new friends. This behavioral response echoes what people often do after disasters like tornadoes and earthquakes or terrorist events like 9/11.[1] Amazingly, it's been three years since the hurricane, and the monkeys continue to seek out and provide social support. Unfortunately, "all for one and one for all" solidarity in humans often fades as people try to put the memory of terrible experiences behind them.

As I write, we're currently living through what are likely the early stages of the COVID-19 pandemic, which may last for many months or years. COVID-19 has led to the implementation of social distancing across the world, causing an abrupt and unprecedented impact on our behavior and our economies. The consequences of these severe disruptions to our social lives are keenly felt in our longing to be together and get back to work. Given what we've discovered about the importance of social support for mitigating extreme stress, the impact of social distancing on our ability to weather this "storm" is profound. As we navigate the COVID-19 "new normal," there is an enormous opportunity, and real imperative, to be better leaders—at the office, in our homes, and in our communities. As we'll discuss, neuroscience can help illuminate this new, enlightened path forward.

How Neuroscience Can Provide the Answers

Two years ago, Wharton neuroscience postdoctoral fellow Feng Sheng and I gathered groups of smartphone users to see if they had an emotional and social connection with their brand. We focused particularly on two of the behemoths that seem to inspire at times fierce battles between their loyalists—Apple and Samsung.

In the case of these two phone giants and many other brands, people talk about them as if they were other people: They love or hate them, and they imbue them with human traits such as creativity, practicality, sexiness, or smartness.

We know how our brains respond to the people we're closely connected to, and we wondered if our brains respond similarly to brands and companies. Because smartphones are such a personal item, we decided to focus on them, recruiting groups of Apple and Samsung users who didn't own products of the other brand.

Participants had their brains scanned with functional magnetic resonance imaging (fMRI) while seeing positive, negative, and neutral messages about both brands. This technique takes snapshots of blood flow in the brain, allowing us to visualize brain activity. Apple users showed empathy for their own brand: The reward-related areas of the brain were activated by good news about Apple, and the pain and negative feeling parts of the brain were activated by bad news. They were neutral about any kind of Samsung news. This is exactly what we see when people empathize with other people—particularly their family and friends—but don't feel the joy and pain of people they don't know.

Samsung users, on the other hand, showed no increased activity in either area when they were shown positive and negative news about their brand. Interestingly, though, the pain areas were activated by good news about Apple, and the reward areas were activated by bad news about the rival company—some serious schadenfreude, or "reverse empathy."

If I were the Chief Marketing Officer of Samsung, I would be worried. Samsung customers' brains tell us they're just not that socially and emotionally connected to the brand, and that makes the company much more vulnerable to a potential competitor (just as a weak workplace culture can lead to higher turnover). Apple, of course, has been building the connection with its customers for years. Its customer experience is consistent across products, the app and retail stores, marketing messages, and website. The experience has deepened over time as new functions and apps allow users to, for example, pay for every purchase, navigate to physical locations, control their home electronics, identify the health value of potential food purchases, and more. It's even indispensable when you're not awake: There are apps that measure your sleep cycle.

What we've learned about how people form connections with brands could be helpful for leaders seeking to improve connections with and among their workforces. And beyond that, neuroscience is helping us discover how different people react to aspects of everyday business. Perhaps most importantly, these studies reveal that traditional methods in business that rely on surveys and self-reporting sometimes fail to capture what's really going on in the minds of our employees and our customers. Neuroscience provides powerful tools and insights that can help leaders bridge this gap to make better decisions.

What Are You Thinking?

Back to the monkeys. Believe it or not, they're the reason I got into the field of neuroscience in the first place. In 1994, I was finishing my PhD in biological anthropology at Penn, conducting research into the foraging skills of monkeys. It was interesting work, but a question kept nagging at me—one that would take me to New York University for the next five years to complete a postdoctoral fellowship in neuroscience. I couldn't stop asking myself, "What are they thinking?" Measuring monkey behavior was one thing. Figuring out what's going on in their brains, and by extension our own brains, became my life's work.

In 2015, after 15 years as a professor and four years as director of the Institute for Brain Sciences at Duke University, I returned to Philadelphia as a University of Pennsylvania Penn Integrates Knowledge professor. I have full appointments in the Perelman School of Medicine's Neuroscience Department, the School of Arts and Sciences' Psychology Department, and Wharton's Marketing Department. I'm also the founding faculty director of the Wharton Neuroscience Initiative, where our goal is to build better business through brain science. The wide array of my appointments shows how deeply pervasive the importance of neuroscience is becoming across disciplines, as more and more industries look for optimal leadership and employee engagement.

Indeed, neuroscience is much more than simply understanding how our brains work. We're forging a new discipline drawing on neuroscience, behavioral science, data science, psychology, economics, marketing, management, evolutionary biology, and anthropology. As director of the initiative, I hope to move neuroscience out of the lab and into the hands of people so they can unlock its full potential at work and in their daily lives. Our goal is to translate our research into direct applications—tools that people can use to reach their peak performance and enhance their well-being and that organizations can use to improve just about everything, from marketing to management to decision-making.

Ten years ago, I didn't think what we're now doing every day was even possible. I never imagined we'd have high-quality brain-monitoring devices that could collect data from people engaged in real-world activities. But today we're using devices of our own design to learn about performance in teams working together in the gym, on the playing field, and in the boardroom. Neuroscience is now making it possible to predict sales across the country by measuring the brain activity of a small number of people watching the same commercial. We can even measure a customer's shopping experience without interrupting them to ask them what they're thinking and feeling. These advances—and many others—give me great confidence that we will continue to see breakthroughs in other domains. We'll better understand how to achieve greater performance, whether in the boardroom or on the playing field, and we'll be able to apply what we learn to create more value for people, for companies, and for society.

Neuroscience is providing answers to many business challenges, such as why two managers, when presented with the same set of information, make very different decisions. We're learning why an idea for a new product generates excitement in a focus group but falls flat when it reaches the market, and why seemingly similar teams produce drastically different work outcomes. We're even learning how some companies build strong social and emotional connections with their customers and why others do not, and our findings suggest neuroscience can account for differences in brand loyalty and ultimately help predict the lifetime value to the company of all the ad spend used to acquire a customer.

How to Read This Book

What does a leader's brain look like? The leader's brain is energized yet taxed. It is focused yet flexible. It is finding insights that can solve seemingly impossible problems. It is making the right decisions. It is finding ways to collaborate with others and foster team chemistry. It is constantly providing feedback and helping people to learn and change their behavior for the better.

The "leader's brain" is a mindset. It is a leadership approach that seeks to use neuroscience insights to develop our skills as managers and leaders. It is my goal that you will be able to use these insights and apply them to your own work, whether it's in how you approach day-to-day management tasks or the broad scope of your vision as a leader. And I hope you will also be able to use these insights to be a leader in your community and to live a happier and healthier life at home.

Today, our pioneering research has already deepened our understanding of how key areas of the brain work and how that understanding can be applied in business settings. I provide an overview of this in chapter 1. We're learning more about the social brain network—an interconnected set of brain areas that manages our interactions with other people—and how it can be strengthened, which I also cover in chapter 1. As our collaborators at the University of Oxford have found, our ability to connect with others is like a muscle: The more you use it, the more it grows.[2] This is a powerful and important message, especially in business, where relationships are so critically important. You don't have to be gregarious, but you can improve social ties by working on them. Talking to people you don't know will physically change your social brain network. As a bonus, you'll not only improve your results but also be healthier and happier.

Findings on the social brain network also provide important insights on key leadership skills such as effective team building and communication, which I cover in chapters 2 and 3. You'll learn what's going on in your brain when your team is working in sync with each other, and how you can tweak *how* you deliver a message to make sure others hear it.

In chapter 4, you'll learn how to encourage greater creativity and innovation, not by hiring new talent but by better motivating your existing team. You'll even learn how to get your customers to love your brand in the same way they love their families. In chapter 5, you'll find out how to make more effective decisions crucial to the future of your company, and in chapter 6, you'll discover how to drive better performance through learning. Finally, in chapter 7, we'll explore a still-untapped potential and where brain science might take leaders to even bigger heights in the future.

This book is all about building a leader's brain to help you enhance your leadership. It's my hope that by exploring cutting-edge neuroscience and its practical applications for business, you'll be able to make important new improvements in your leadership capabilities, the performance and job satisfaction of your team, and work outcomes.

And you might have some fun doing it.

Michael Platt
Philadelphia

Chapter 1

Leadership Is About Relationships
Building Connections with the Social Brain

R eady for an exam? We're going to take the E test. Snap your fingers five times quickly with your writing hand. Then, with your index finger, draw a capital E on your forehead.

If you drew it so someone else could read it (the open side of the E is facing to your left), you're more likely to consider the perspectives of others. If you drew it so you could read it, you tend to be self-oriented and less interested in others' perspectives.

This test, developed by Wharton management professor Maurice Schweitzer and coauthor Adam Galinsky, was designed to determine who is more likely to be "boss material" and who isn't. But the test, published in Schweitzer and Galinsky's book *Friend & Foe: When to Cooperate, When to Compete, and How to Succeed at Both*,[3] has another takeaway.

"Power blinds us to the plight of others," the authors said. "And this 'blindness' can have serious consequences. It can lead the powerful to lose their kingdom."[4]

Not taking others' perspectives also turns down what's known as your *social brain*. Those below you in a hierarchy may have valuable ideas, opinions, and insights that you can't access if you're too self-oriented.

Relationships are key to business success. That's good news, because humans—like monkeys, crows, groundhogs, and other animals—are biologically specialized to connect with others. In fact, there is a direct relationship between social integration and survival: Relationships provide safety, a buffer from stress, and other biological advantages.

The meta study "Social Relationships and Mortality Risk," by researchers at Brigham Young University and the University of North Carolina at Chapel Hill, found a "50% increased likelihood of survival for participants with stronger social relationships, regardless of age, sex, initial health status, and even cause of death."[5] Strong social connections have also been linked to lower risks for high blood pressure, stroke, and heart attacks.

But we're not just healthier—we're also happier when we have strong social connections. One study concluded that making connections with others results in lower rates of anxiety and depression,[6] and—as you'll soon see when we look closely at the social brain network—relationships help us better regulate our emotions. At work, studies show when we connect socially with others we're more productive and engaged, better at cooperating, more likely to be promoted, and even more successful at starting new ventures. In short, we are more satisfied, and we make more money.

The opposite is also true. A lack of social connections—loneliness—results in lower engagement and higher absenteeism and turnover rates. The negative effects of the stress that loneliness puts on the body are equivalent to smoking a pack of cigarettes a day.[7]

The Leadership Link

Leadership is a set of abilities that only a lucky few are born with. They're the natural relationship builders, master negotiators and persuaders, agile and strategic thinkers, and seekers of new perspectives, ideas, and voices. The good news for the rest of us is that those abilities can be developed, as Google discovered with Project Oxygen.

Google began the project in 2008 to figure out what makes a great manager. The results forced the company to rethink its entire process of management training and selection. Google learned from its workforce that great managers were not necessarily the people being promoted—those with strong technical skills. Instead, the best managers had strong social skills.

Google identified eight behaviors that great managers have in common, such as good coaching and supporting career development, and then trained managers on them. A 2018 article on the company's blog reported the results: "an improvement in management at Google and team outcomes like turnover, satisfaction, and performance over time."[8]

During the years Google was working to develop strong managerial social skills, neuroscientists made a remarkable discovery: Each of us possesses a "social brain network," a collection of brain areas that work together to allow us to interact with other people.[9] This means we are no longer restricted to asking people about their own social skills when evaluating them for a leadership position or as a member of a team. We have an unbiased and objective way to identify who has strong skills, who would benefit from improving them, and which interventions and training are most likely to pay off.

Breakthroughs in neuroscience have identified the brain mechanisms that support our ability to connect and communicate with others—the social brain network—and reveal how we can strengthen it. Other research into our visual system and its connection to the brain has revealed just how little we perceive of our sensory environment and how that narrow view can lead to assumptions and biases. Left unchecked, these assumptions and biases can adversely influence our effectiveness at creating and developing new ideas, along with our ability to lead, manage, negotiate, and build relationships with colleagues and clients. We will explore steps that can be taken to develop your social brain.

The Social Brain and the "Superbrain"

Both the size of the areas making up the social brain network and the robustness of the wiring between these areas are directly correlated with your ability to make social connections. By measuring these parameters, neuroscientists can predict with startling accuracy how many relationships you have.

Neuroscience research shows you can be born with a strong or weak social brain network. People who suffer impairments in their ability to connect with others, such as those with autism or schizophrenia, show real differences in their social brain networks. But recent research in monkeys reveals that it's not all destiny. You can also enlarge your social brain network and make the connections between neurons more dense. How? *By using it.*

Researchers at Oxford showed that when monkeys were challenged to get along with more monkeys, the size of the social brain network and connections within it actually grew.[10] And we know that a larger, more connected social brain network is a key factor in how well we manage our interactions with others.

Thalia Wheatley, a professor of psychological and brain science at Dartmouth, has studied human brains to better understand how they behave in a social context.[11] Her research involves simultaneously scanning people's brains as they talk to each other while lying inside MRI machines in different rooms, a method known as hyperscanning. The findings demonstrate that when we communicate and connect, our brains continuously adjust and adapt to each other. Wheatley says that when people "put their heads together," they create something greater than the sum of their parts—what she calls the "superbrain" or "ubermind."[12]

While two or more brains working together creates both individual and collective benefits, the opposite is also true. In a recent study, mice that were removed from their communities and placed in isolation showed signs of brain damage.[13] After one month, their neurons had shrunk by about 20%. Levels of the protein BDNF, a catalyst for neural growth, were reduced, and there was more broken DNA in their neurons. As Wheatley noted, "That's a hint that it's not just that we like interaction. It's important to keep us healthy and sane."[14]

Hormones like oxytocin also enhance social brain function. Sometimes referred to as the "love hormone," oxytocin can be traced back to the earliest animals with backbones. In mammals, its primary role is to cement the bond between mother and infant (it's released during childbirth and nursing). But it can also turn up connections between other people, and it's showing great promise as a therapy for social impairments in disorders like autism.

Oxytocin is also released in the brain when we receive a gentle touch. In other words, a hug can actually deepen our relationship with someone on a biochemical level. This might help explain, for example, why athletes often embrace in the huddle. Eye contact also releases oxytocin, which is even true between humans and dogs.[15] When you take a break from reading this book, look your dog in the eye—you'll both get an oxytocin boost, a great tune-up before socializing with others.

The message is clear. At the end of a long workweek, you could spend Saturday and Sunday bingeing your favorite show on Netflix. Or, you could get out and engage with others, exercising your social brain by talking to people at the farmer's market or community picnic. Doing this every weekend will boost the structure and function of your social brain network and make you better at relating to other people—both at home and at work.

These practices can be challenging, if not impossible, while practicing social distancing to slow down the spread of infectious diseases like COVID-19. Although technology has made it possible to interact with each other and our teams using apps like Zoom and BlueJeans, the limitations of videoconferencing are often painfully clear. Online video often obscures the tiny muscle contractions, known as microexpressions, that continuously play out across our faces as we interact with others. Poor video resolution and variation in lighting can also mask changes in pupil size that track our engagement and interest. Moreover, the geometric offset between the location of the camera on a computer and the eyes of the person on-screen frustrates mutual gaze, which is an important component of normal face-to-face interactions. All these challenges are intensified when multiple people are on-screen in tiny "Brady Bunch" windows. For these reasons, remote teamwork and videoconferencing often feel exhausting—not just for leaders and their teams but for teachers and students too.

One solution is to take breaks from videoconferencing and rely on purely audio conference calls instead. Although you'll miss out on some of the nonverbal cues we normally rely on to navigate communication, at least you won't be mentally taxed or confused trying to read and interpret distorted visual social information.

How to Develop Your Social Brain

To make a connection and develop your social brain, it's critical to understand what's going on during social interactions. The key to managing that connection in any interaction is simply to pay attention to the other person. There are two key ways to do that.

Watch and Learn

You need to take in sensory information and make sense of it. That includes observing facial expressions, which scientists tell us are universal (and even extend to other mammals—when monkeys or rats taste something bitter, they make the same expression we do).[16] In fact, the only reason we make these facial expressions is to communicate with others. If you spend meetings looking at your phone instead of the people around you, you're starving your social brain network of the information it needs to make sense of others. The same holds true when you're on a Zoom call and you're texting on your phone.

Visual information (as well as other sensory information, such as what we hear other people say) is passed on to the social brain network, which then extracts meaning from it. If you're seeing a person, for example, you will interpret their facial expressions, note where they are looking, sense their emotional state, and create a mental model of the individual. This model asks, What are they doing? What are they likely to do next? What do they want? What do they know? Will they cooperate with me or try to deceive me?

Reading the Mind in the Eyes

How well can you read emotions in the eyes of others? The Reading the Mind in the Eyes assessment tool was developed by University of Cambridge professor Simon Baron-Cohen to test levels of empathy and EQ, or emotional intelligence. Baron-Cohen has used the test with adults with high-functioning autism and Asperger's syndrome to measure variations in social sensitivity. Studies using fMRI have shown that the social brain network is typically activated during the exercise. You can take the test at http://socialintelligence.labinthewild.org/mite.

Take Someone Else's Perspective

The next step in understanding another person is perspective-taking, which involves putting yourself in someone else's shoes to understand things from their vantage point. Because we are hardwired to see things through a social lens, we need to make sense of what we're seeing by creating a story about it. And to tell a story that makes sense, we need to ensure our perspective-taking skills are in order.

As it turns out, perspective-taking has its fair share of pitfalls. In the remainder of the chapter, I review some of them.

Know the Challenges with Perspective-Taking in Order to Mitigate Them

For most people, perspective-taking is a fundamental and effortless skill. As cognitive function develops over the first few years of life, young children develop a deeper understanding of what another person finds important, pays attention to, believes, or wants. This ability to see the world from another's point of view is a key component of social interactions. When perspective-taking goes awry in development, it is often the sign of serious problems such as autism and schizophrenia, and the lack of this vital skill can lead to catastrophic consequences. But there are other, more subtle ways in which our ability to take the perspective of others can be diminished, including by unconsciously held biases and feelings of power.

Our Brains Can Be Tricked

Remarkably, some of the brain areas that help us make sense of other people and understand their intentions and experience can also activate when we're observing or interacting with inanimate objects—when those objects move in a way that seems social. Hollywood directors often hijack our social brains by using cinematography that encourages us to take the visual perspective of inanimate objects and, in doing so, empathize with their experience.

Think that sounds far-fetched? Go to YouTube and watch the IKEA commercial directed by Spike Jonze.[17] Was your social brain activated? Then search for "The Heider-Simmel Illusion," a simple animated film that has been used in a number of studies. Created by Smith College experimental psychologists Fritz Heider and Marianne Simmel in 1944, the film was shown to students and they were asked to describe what they saw. Most of the participants said the simple shapes moving around the screen were people, and they created stories about how and why they "interacted." More recently, an fMRI study showed that the "mirror neuron" system, which overlaps with part of the social brain, was activated in people who watched this film. Mirror neurons were first discovered in monkeys, and they are important for understanding others' goals. These neurons are unusual because they respond whenever an individual intentionally reaches out to grab something and when that individual observes another individual reach out, intentionally, to grab the object. These neurons don't respond when a robot or inanimate object performs the same behavior. Activation of the mirror neuron system reflects our tendency to infer the goals and intentions of the people around us—and for some of us this can even extend to objects like our cars or computers.[18]

A Cautionary Tale of Power: GE's Jeffrey Immelt

Studies of both humans and monkeys show that the more power (real or perceived) you have, the less attention you pay to others, especially those of lower status. Being or believing you are higher status than someone else turns down the activity in your social brain, making you less attentive and thereby less likely to take the perspective of others. This makes it difficult to understand their goals and intentions, and makes it more challenging to cooperate. It can also cause you to miss signals and other forms of information that are important for successful social interactions. One way to avoid these pitfalls is to emphasize equality and respect for everyone, no matter their status. In business, this can be institutionalized by implementing a flatter organizational structure.[19]

Ari Weinzweig, the CEO and cofounder of Zingerman's gourmet food company, relies on collective decision-making rather than the standard corporate hierarchy to help with perspective-taking and its benefits. He opens executive meetings—and the company's books—to all employees.[20] One study suggests that this level of openness to the perspectives and ideas of others makes him more influential than those who follow more traditional, rigid leadership models.[21] Openness also provides access to information that would otherwise be unavailable to leaders. In a standard corporate hierarchy, those on the lower rungs have no incentive to share their ideas, and indeed are often discouraged from doing so. As an interesting aside, Wheatley found that influential leaders come from more diverse countries, counties, and cities, which may help them more easily see things from the perspective of others.[22]

Perspective-taking doesn't appear to have been part of the equation when Jeffrey Immelt, the former CEO of General Electric, spent $10.6 billion to acquire the power and grid unit of French company Alstom in 2015.[23] At the time, Immelt called it a "significant step in GE's transformation," claiming it would "further our core industrial growth." Immelt pushed the deal through despite a number of disturbing signals and warnings he chose to ignore.

GE's board of directors was warned before he was chosen as CEO that his signature optimism was a weakness that had led him to overpay before.[24] Those fears were not unfounded. Under Immelt, GE spent $11 billion in 2010–2011 buying oil and gas industry businesses—then crude prices fell in 2014.

While Immelt was still considering the acquisition, Alstom's 2014 annual report noted that "excess capacity in developed markets" was a concern for its power business.[25] Internally, some of GE's directors and advisors were wary. Immelt pushed on, even as European and American regulators pressured GE to concede some of Alstom's most profitable programs and business units to competitors, making the deal significantly less attractive. Immelt eventually led GE to make the most expensive industrial purchase in the company's history.

Today, Immelt is gone, and the Alstom deal is, by all accounts, a disaster. GE's power division is its most troubled, and, adding insult to injury, France recently fined GE $57 million, claiming the company never created the French jobs it promised.[26]

Our Brains Have Biases

Power isn't the only thing that can make us less attentive and less able to take the perspective of others. Several studies have found a strong "group identification effect" that is the source of implicit bias against members of outside groups. Even when people say they empathize equally with members of their own group, based on race, religion, political party, and other groups, brain scans show that this is not true. Activity in the parts of the social brain that underlie empathy is not as robust when we interact with members of other groups. This bias is not necessarily conscious but most likely represents the way our brains get "tuned" by the diversity of the people we interact with most while growing up. Our own sense of identity strongly reflects what we've learned, implicitly, about the groups in which we grew up.

Neuroscience also shows that this bias can be reduced, because some factors that contribute to identity and who is included in our "tribe" are malleable. Think of a sporting event in which fans of a team are different ethnically, socioeconomically, and politically. But when they all put on the same jerseys, they come together as one group. Focusing on shared goals and values, like "our" team's performance, flattens other biases and allows people who differ from one another in many ways to connect. (There's much more on team building in chapter 3.) This is vividly revealed by scans showing increased activity in areas underlying empathy when people from different ethnic groups focus on being on the same team.

Scientists are using these findings to create tools for reducing bias. In one study, people watched the face of a person from a different ethnic group on a screen being stroked with a cotton swab while their own faces were stroked at the same time.[27] This experience tended to reduce implicit bias toward the other ethnic group, because the participant's brain integrated what they saw and what they felt into their sense of identity. In another study, white rats that were raised with black rats were found to help black rats in distress. White rats raised with only other white rats wouldn't help the black rats. White rats raised with both white rats and black rats helped rats of both colors.[28] It's important to realize that our default processing about who to empathize with reflects what we learned about our tribes growing up, but this can be changed and research continues to identify new ways to reduce bias.

Do You Lead How You Eat?

We all know that what we eat affects our physical fitness. It also affects many of the biochemical processes that influence our behavior. New studies link a lack of protein during breakfast with depleted blood levels of the amino acid precursor for dopamine, a chemical that signals reward and is important for learning and decision-making.[29] In one study, people were more likely to reject an unfair financial offer (therefore receiving nothing) if they had a carb-rich breakfast. Those who ate a lower-carb, higher-protein breakfast were more likely to take the money.

In another study, people were given a high-protein breakfast, a low-protein breakfast, or no breakfast and were then tested for dopamine markers. Those who ate the high-protein breakfast had a 15-fold increase in blood levels of the amino acid precursor for dopamine.[30] In another study, administering a drug that temporarily *increased* dopamine in the brain caused participants to make more equitable decisions toward others.[31] This finding directly shows that increasing dopamine levels in the brain affects social decisions in much the same way that eating a protein-rich breakfast does. More generally, a large study of thousands of people found that how much tyrosine people included in their diet predicted cognitive performance—independent of age.[32]

Of course, given the often back-and-forth scientific advice on the effects of different foods on the health of our bodies (remember when eggs were bad?), we should take this work with a grain of salt. But it does vividly illustrate the fact that our brains don't only demand lots of energy (about 20% of the calories we eat) but also need specific nutrients to work properly. Ultimately, you can't go wrong by eating a well-balanced diet.

The Leader's Brainwaves: Things to Remember

- How well we connect with others is key to leading them. We can strengthen the social brain by increasing our understanding of sensory cues and taking others' perspectives.
- Keep power in check: Studies show that the more powerful you are or even feel, the less attention you pay to others (especially those a few rungs beneath you on the corporate hierarchy). This makes it difficult to take their perspectives and learn valuable new information.
- Biases can hinder perspective-taking and the ability to empathize. Being cognizant of us-versus-them thinking, and instead focusing on commonalities, can help reduce the effects of biases.

Chapter 2

Brains That Fire Together
Wire Together
The Secrets of Team Chemistry

It was an unseasonably warm day in Lake Placid, New York, on February 22, 1980. Temperatures reached 50 degrees outside the Olympic Arena, where the US men's hockey team faced the Soviet Union. To call the Soviets the favorites was a vast understatement: They were widely considered the best team in the world, with gold medals from the previous four Olympics and a roster filled with full-time professional athletes, including four of the game's all-time best players.

US coach Herb Brooks's years of experience told him his team, made up of college-age amateurs, would need more than just talent to beat the Soviets. Drawing on his background in psychology, he intentionally set out to build a team with extraordinary chemistry. Tryouts included a mandatory 300-question psychological test to determine "mental toughness" and to reveal which players had more in common in terms of temperament. He then selected two groups of players who had been teammates before (nine of them for him at the University of Minnesota). Brooks also decided to be tougher than usual, believing that the players would bond over their dislike of him.

During months of training, Brooks instilled in those players the belief that, although underdogs, they had what it took to win. On the morning of the game, he told them, "It's meant to be. This is your moment and it's going to happen."[33] It was his highly intentional building and fostering of team chemistry that has been credited with the win: US 4, Soviet Union 3. Later dubbed the "Miracle on Ice," it's considered one of the greatest moments in US sports history.

Since that game, Brooks's methods have been studied and written about as a model for team leadership. Luckily, very few leaders adopt the bond-by-hating-me method. But not enough leaders work as Brooks did to intentionally build team chemistry. In fact, many of the problems with today's teams can be traced to leaders who put teams together, give them a shared task, and hope for the best.

There Is No "I" in "Team"

Teamwork has never been easy. Teams can waste time and resources. They can be slow and underperform. They can be dysfunctional. And today, they must contend with many new challenges: They're less stable, with people moving in and out more quickly, and there are geographic, cultural, and communication differences that can impair performance. All these issues can be even more problematic when teams must work together virtually.

But teams are still responsible for most of the work in organizations, and some of them do it quite well. The problem, it seems, isn't with teams themselves—it's with the ways they're run. Building on neuroscience findings on the social brains of individuals, new research has focused on team chemistry, and the insights for both team leaders and team members are powerful.

Through extensive studies on team effectiveness, Wharton management professor Martine Haas has identified more precisely what chemistry entails. She and coauthor Mark Mortensen wrote in *Harvard Business Review* that the basics of team effectiveness identified by former Harvard psychology professor J. Richard Hackman in the early 2000s (compelling direction, strong structure, and supportive context) remain important. But they also found that modern teams also require a fourth condition: a shared mindset. They say this can be achieved when team leaders "foster a common identity and common understanding."[34]

But when a team has a common identity and understanding, what's going on among the members? And, more importantly, what can team leaders do to achieve it? Research and insights from neuroscience are giving us answers to those key questions.

Synchrony Is the Secret Sauce of Teamwork

A key finding relates to what we covered in the previous chapter about the social brain network. When people have a strong connection with each other, or are cooperating well together during a task, their brains go into synchrony: patterns of neuronal activity become aligned. And when their brains go into synchrony, other physiological processes, like their heart rates, also go into synchrony. Neuroscientists have found that physiological synchrony increases liking, understanding, empathy, rapport, and cooperation.[35] It also allows you to communicate more information and promotes greater understanding—all important for team chemistry.

There have been numerous studies of synchronous physiology between mothers and their infants, teachers and their students, and even firewalkers and the audiences that observe them stepping across hot coals.[36] In a study published in 2017, an electroencephalogram (EEG) was used to measure brain activity in students and a teacher at a New York City high school.[37] When there was greater synchrony among students and with their teacher, researchers observed higher engagement and greater performance.

How did they achieve that synchrony? In the high school case, it's tied to attention and activating the social brain: The best predictor of brain synchrony was whether students sustained eye contact with each other during the two minutes *before* class. This is obviously more difficult to achieve in an online setting. Classes held on platforms like Zoom afford some degree of access to another person's attention and facial expressions, but the effect is only as good as the technology that renders it. There are hardware issues too: When participants look at the camera located at the top of the screen, they're not looking at the other people in attendance. Today's urgency to find better ways to connect and collaborate remotely is driving innovative efforts to address these concerns. It's important that we devote intense research into finding out how to boost synchrony in remote teams working together, apart, via teleconferencing apps.

In early 2019, Norihiro Sadato of the National Institute for Physiological Sciences in Japan determined exactly what was going on in those two crucial minutes of eye contact in the NYC high school.[38] Using fMRI, he and his colleagues showed that eye contact prepares the social brain to understand the intentions and actions of others. It activates the same areas of both people's brains at the same time: the cerebellum and the mirror neuron system. These areas are activated both when we move parts of our body (eyes included) and when we observe someone moving theirs.

But eye contact is just the start. Team leaders can move the brain that's *prepared* for synchrony *into* synchrony in a number of ways. Recently, my research team and I visited Penn's Coach Ted A. Nash Land Based Rowing Center to see if different training conditions generate different levels of synchrony and higher performance. We focused on heart rate synchrony, because it's relatively cheap and easy to measure in sweaty athletes. Ultimately, synchronized heart rates reflect a cascading process that begins in the brain and percolates down to other physiological processes, which can be measured by wearables like Fitbits or Apple watches. In our study, we used Polar chest straps to get the most accurate measure of heart rate possible.

First, we tested individual crew members rowing alone on ergometers (or, as rowers call indoor rowing machines, "ergs"). Next, we tested all four teammates rowing next to each other in a line of ergs. Finally, we connected the ergs with a long rod that forced the team to row in physical synchrony, which we hypothesized would force their brains into synchrony by experiencing the same sensations and actions at the same time.

While the study is ongoing, our initial findings support the idea that physical synchrony leads to brain synchrony. On a crew team, in which physical synchrony is necessary not just to win but also to keep the boat from tipping over, this would be a major finding. Our early results also suggest that just seeing and hearing (and possibly smelling!) your fellow teammates helps generate physiological synchrony. Crew members who rowed alongside each other showed nearly the same heart rate synchrony as those forced to row in sync, while those who rowed alone were completely out of sync. Importantly, synchronized heart rates were strongly associated with group flow—a sensation of connection and oneness that rowers call "swing." Coaches could use this type of information to create training sessions that deepen team connections. They could even use it to put the right people together on a team.

We're also studying a soccer team in the United Kingdom to help us understand the factors that predict on-field performance. We are hoping to use the data to fine-tune the training programs teams use and to help coaches make better management decisions that lead to the best team chemistry. Why so much focus on sports? Sports is an ideal petri dish in which to try out these ideas, because the outcome measures are easily quantified, and small improvements in performance can have a major impact on winning or losing.

Our findings generalize from the playing field to the boardroom. We're currently conducting a study in which we are measuring physiological synchrony in the heart rates of people on committees of three to six members who are evaluating job candidates for a position in their hypothetical company. Each committee member has access to both shared and unique information about the candidate. What we're finding is that committees with higher physiological synchrony are more likely to reach consensus by sharing their unique insights, and these committees ultimately decide on the right candidate. Whether that can be replicated in committees working remotely, as so many have transitioned to doing amid the pandemic, is a subject of current study in my lab.

Back at the office, it turns out that those team-building exercises aren't necessarily a waste of time (seriously—Google "team building" and "waste" to see dozens of pages' worth of hits). A number of studies show that brain synchrony can occur in a group that's working on the same puzzle, building a structure with Legos, or even watching the same movie.[39] As we saw earlier in the high school study, one way to boost synchrony is through eye contact, which may synchronize brains through the release of oxytocin. Supporting this idea, when we administered oxytocin to monkeys, their behavior became more synchronous, which might in turn generate even greater brain synchrony.[40]

Today, though, the amount of time individuals engage in social interactions with those outside their household has plummeted, while the amount of time spent in virtual interactions, especially in work-related encounters, has increased dramatically. The consequences of these severe disruptions to our social and professional lives on decision-making and mental well-being, potentially via reduced social synchrony, are not yet known. New research can help us understand these impacts and their mechanisms, and it may also illuminate our way through the COVID-19 crisis and enable us to adapt to future crises that require collective action, such as climate change or future pandemics.

Three Ways to Promote Synchrony

Playing Games

The Helium Hoop activity requires teams of six to eight people to work in physical synchrony to complete a task. Team members place their index fingers on the underside of a hula hoop. The group then attempts to evenly lower the hoop to the ground, quickly realizing that it's impossible without a cohesive effort.

Debriefing the activity should highlight not just performance feedback on the task but also the group's strengths and weaknesses. We are currently investigating Helium Hoop in the lab to determine the neurobiological mechanisms that support better performance.

Storytelling

Encouraging group synchrony can also be done through storytelling, according to research by Princeton University neuroscientist Uri Hasson.[41] That meeting where you recap a job well done does much more than simply boost morale—you're actually syncing your team and preparing for the next win.

Mirroring

The next time you meet with your team, need to defuse a tense situation, or enter into a negotiation, try mirroring. This typically unconscious behavior, subtly copying the body movements of someone else, isn't just about body language or mimicry: It's wired into the brain to establish rapport and connection. The use of fMRI shows that brain synchrony occurs between the person mirroring and the person being mirrored.

As a team leader, when you mirror gestures or even emotional responses, you signal to your team that you understand and connect with them. It's a nonverbal signal of trust and support, and it also helps lower the tension in a stressful situation. If you're trying to intercede in a disagreement between two or more members, repeat what you hear each person say in a neutral tone (don't let your voice betray criticism or disagreement). This can allow each party—and you—to better understand where everyone is coming from.

Mirroring language works in negotiations too. Former FBI agent Chris Voss shared in *Never Split the Difference*, a book he coauthored, that when words, voice tone, and body movements are in sync, people feel less threatened and are more willing to open up. Voss specifically repeated one to three keywords in the last sentence spoken by the other person during negotiations, describing the technique as one of the quickest ways to establish rapport.[42]

How to Hack Team Identity

When Warby Parker brings on new hires, it provides both tangible and intangible elements that represent the company and its team culture. They include a copy of Jack Kerouac's *The Dharma Bums* (the company was named after Kerouac characters), Martin's pretzels (the founders often ate them when they were establishing the company), and a gift certificate for a Thai restaurant (it was the only one open late at night when the company was in its early days).[43]

Team relationships flourish when we build or focus on commonalities. That means creating a team identity that everyone can believe in. Leaders strengthen empathy, mutual understanding, and a willingness to cooperate when we feel we're on the same team. If we believe someone is not a member, the opposite is true: We distrust them and find it difficult, if not impossible, to collaborate.

Neuroscience research shows we're wired to make that friend-or-foe decision as soon as we come into contact with someone. Thus, team leaders should work to set the stage for connections as quickly as possible, reducing the chance of a "foe response" and increasing feelings of trust. Research by Jay Van Bavel, a professor at New York University, reveals that people can often cooperate on a team even when they have been a member for just a few minutes.[44]

Multiple studies using brain scans showed that people perceive others more positively when they have been told they are in their group.[45] This response is common even when the other person is of a different sex or race. Oxytocin works similarly. The hormone is released when we build strong personal connections, minimizing the threat response and enabling us to view another as a friend and fellow team member.

Even on teams that come together to complete a short-term project, it makes sense to establish team identity through shared goals, values, and vision. Those shared beliefs amplify trust and understanding. Everyone needs to understand at the outset what the team plans to accomplish, how that goal could not be accomplished by any one individual, and what's important for achieving it.

Studies on the brain's reward centers have found that they are activated when team members see their team, and other members on it, do well. Hitting benchmarks, individual achievements, and other positive outcomes should be common knowledge on a team. That same activation happens when we work well with others, which means our brains are wired to lead us into cooperation. It was, and maybe still is, the best way to make sure we keep our place in our tribe.

Team Chemistry Wins the World Series

While establishing connections quickly is important, so is maintaining them. Team leaders should continuously consider chemistry between members as they make decisions that affect the team. When the long-shot San Francisco Giants won Major League Baseball's World Series in 2012 against the Detroit Tigers, they quickly became the object of team chemistry researcher interest, much like the Miracle on Ice hockey team. Statistically, they were nothing special. They had the fifth-best batting average in baseball but were 15th in RBIs and last in home runs. They had one potential Hall of Fame player, compared with the Tigers' three.

What happened to make them wipe out the Tigers in a 4–0 series sweep? Two events provide clues. A few months before the playoffs, the Giants' Melky Cabrera, the league's All-Star Game MVP, was suspended for 50 games for taking performance-enhancing drugs. He could have rejoined the team for the postseason, but manager Bruce Bochy and general manager Brian Sabean decided instead to substitute in Gregor Blanco, a decent outfielder who was with the Giants on a minor-league deal.

Why make such a risky decision? Bochy and Sabean felt the real risk was the damage to team chemistry that would have occurred if Cabrera came back. And they were vindicated. Blanco played brilliant defense, and his RBI triple in Game 3 proved to be decisive.

The other event was described by pitcher Barry Zito, who told *The Atlantic* about the team's turning point when they were down two games to zero in the first round of playoffs.[46] After Bochy finished his pregame talk, midseason acquisition Hunter Pence decided to speak. According to Zito, Pence had the passion of a preacher at a revival meeting, urging a rebirth of the team. He also made "feverish" eye contact with his fellow teammates (oxytocin at work again).

Chemistry Creators

At the 2017 MIT Sloan Sports Analytics Conference, two economists from the Federal Reserve Bank of Chicago and an assistant professor at the Kelley School of Business at Indiana University presented "In Search of David Ross," a paper on quantifying team chemistry.[47] The authors studied over 15 seasons of data on teams whose win-loss record was vastly different from what would be predicted by looking at individual performance alone. What they found was a number of players who were on teams that regularly overperformed. The researchers hypothesized that these players, by creating chemistry, were able to lift their teams up to perform at much higher levels than individual contributions would suggest.

In baseball, these "chemistry creators" are not the superstars that cost teams tens of millions of dollars a year. Instead, on the surface they look like a majority of players with decent, but not standout, statistics. And that means they're often undervalued. When working for the Red Sox, assistant general manager Jed Hoyer drafted first baseman Anthony Rizzo, who spent most of the next five years playing on minor league teams. In 2012, with the Chicago Cubs, Hoyer negotiated a trade for Rizzo from the San Diego Padres. He knew what he was doing.

Rizzo, who still plays for the Cubs, is considered one of those chemistry creators (in addition to now being an All-Star player). In 2016, when his team was down three games to one in the World Series against the Cleveland Indians, Rizzo decided the team needed more than pep talks. Before each of the final three games, he danced naked to the theme from *Rocky*, a ritual that the aforementioned

Ross says kept the team's nerves at bay. The Cubs won those next three games, and their first World Series since 1908.

MLB consultant and child psychologist Russell Carleton has also studied team chemistry and says acts like Rizzo's dance create connections. Researchers at Berkeley have gone a step further. They installed GoPro cameras in the dugout of a Giants minor league team to determine whether there's a connection between fist bumps, high fives, and other ritualized contact. Their findings could be another example of the connection between physical synchrony and brain synchrony.[48]

In one analysis, Carleton showed that teams with less turnover hit more home runs.[49] A number of studies by Gallup confirm the link between turnover and performance: When team members feel connected to one another, they score in the top 20% for engagement and have 59% less turnover.[50] These are findings for team leaders to consider. The solid performer who keeps meetings lively but on track, who makes connections with other team members a priority, and who rises above petty drama is worth cultivating and retaining.

Be a Team Builder

Could your team benefit from stronger bonds and greater cooperation? Team leaders can build identity, and encourage compassion and empathy in the brain, in a number of ways.

Create a Team Identity

Because we are wired to make quick decisions about who's in our tribe and who's not, building team identity should start immediately. Wharton management professor Martine Haas, who has extensively studied both colocated and virtual teams,[51] offers three suggestions that are especially helpful when leading teams of remote workers:

1. Have regular meetings and check-ins where everyone is included and heard, and their inputs and achievements are

recognized as valuable. Daily check-ins have been particularly useful for my own teams as we shifted to remote work
during the pandemic.

2. Make sure everyone understands the team's goals, and continuously remind them of their progress and their importance to the organization as a whole. During our check-ins,
I remind my own teams of their goals and how they contribute to our overall performance and objectives.

3. Virtual office tours and social activities can help workers get
to know one another better and appreciate the realities of
remote working for each member. As we moved to remote
work, every Friday my teammates and I have gathered on
Zoom to play online games. It seems silly, but it works—and
no one skips Friday check-in.

Spend Time Together in Person When Possible

Studies show that in-person contact is important for group cohe-
siveness. First, let's go back to the power of brain synchrony and
activating the social brain: That begins with eye contact. When
you're delivering a critical communication, like your team's goals
and purpose, it's even more important. Much of your effectiveness
is tied to nonverbal cues,[52] which can't be conveyed in an email or
conference call. And, as we've all experienced, this is really difficult
to achieve while working remotely, even using advanced teleconferencing technology.

Get a "Helper's High"

The benefits of volunteering, sometimes referred to as a "helper's
high," for individuals are well known, including stronger social connections, reduced stress levels, and even lower blood pressure. When
you volunteer as a team, those benefits expand. The shared experience of volunteering helps reinforce the empathetic wiring of your
brain and create a shared mindset. That effect continues even when

you are simply reminded of a previous volunteering event. You might also consider wearing team T-shirts during the experience: Research shows that wearing the same team colors can boost the brain's empathy response to people from different ethnic groups.[53]

The Leader's Brainwaves: Things to Remember

- Tribalism is baked into our brains, and we are wired to decide very quickly who's in and who's out. Team leaders need to act quickly to help members feel connected to one another and reduce us-versus-them thinking.
- Practices like eye contact, mirroring, and behavioral synchrony can help build bonds and establish trust. This takes extra effort and attention when working remotely, which can be tiring, so make sure to build in rest between virtual meetings.
- Communication is key. During regularly scheduled meetings, make sure everyone knows your team's goal, keep them apprised of your progress, and encourage team members to share ideas and accomplishments. This is even more important when working remotely, especially when so many younger workers live alone, with fewer real-life connections.

Chapter 3

Say What You Need to Say
Steps to Clearer Communication

O n the night of April 20, 2010, the Deepwater Horizon oil rig was pumping in the Gulf of Mexico for the oil and gas company BP when a surge of natural gas traveled up from the well onto the rig's platform. The rig exploded, killing 11 workers and injuring 17. What followed was the worst oil spill in US history: By the time the well was capped 87 days later, an estimated 206 million gallons of oil had leaked into the Gulf.

The federal commission tasked with investigating the disaster concluded that "the most significant failure . . . and the clear root cause of the blowout, was a failure of industry management." It cited lapses in communication within BP and between the company and its contractors as one of the most significant management errors.[54]

But failing to share information with contractors was just one of BP's strategic communication mistakes. In the weeks following the disaster, the company became, as one news outlet dubbed it, "a textbook example of how not to handle PR."[55] CEO Tony Hayward not only failed to apologize or acknowledge concern about the harm his company caused; he stood on a Louisiana beach in a starched white shirt and dress shoes and blamed others, saying he just wanted to "get my life back."[56]

Luckily, few of us have been in Hayward's position. But most have had the experience of sending an email or text to someone that was completely misunderstood, sometimes with embarrassing or grave consequences. Face-to-face communication is usually more effective, but can still end up giving the wrong impression or failing to convey what we want it to. A better understanding of communication can go a long way toward improving our interactions with others, with obvious benefits for both business and daily life.

If we start at the beginning, with the origins of human language, it's clear that we have lived in communities that depend on social interactions and cooperation to survive. Multiple forms of communication (pointing and other gestures, making sounds) were there from the start, and those communications developed into language.

That means everything we learned about the social brain network in chapter 2 is relevant here too. Think of it this way: All communication is social, so improving communication depends at least in part on strengthening the social brain and connecting well with others. (Remember synchrony and mirroring?)

New neuroscience findings have also added to our knowledge of what defines effective communication. We have learned specific ways that you can fine-tune your message—whether it's giving performance feedback, persuading your team to embrace a change initiative, or selling a product or service—to make sure others listen, attend to the message, and act on it.

One Story, Two Very Different Messages

When communication is effective, the speaker and listeners exhibit synchronized brain waves. As we discussed in chapter 2, that synchrony predicts engagement and learning—exactly what we want from our listeners. Beyond eye contact and mirroring, though, how can we craft messages that increase the chances our listeners' brains will synchronize with our own?

I mentioned that storytelling is one way to encourage group synchrony, strengthening team chemistry in the process. But group synchrony is also important when you want that group to embrace an idea.

In a study by Yaara Yeshurun and colleagues at Princeton University,[57] participants listened to an audio recording of a J. D. Salinger short story called "Pretty Mouth and Green My Eyes." Salinger deliberately made the story ambiguous, leaving readers with at least two different interpretations of what happened. In the story, a jealous husband calls his best friend for reassurance, and his friend is in the embrace of an attractive woman. In one interpretation, the woman is merely a lover; in the other, she is the protagonist's wife.

In the study, participants were divided into two groups, each of which was primed with a one-sentence explanation to accept one of the different frames. Using fMRI, the researchers found that among a group with the same interpretation of the story, neural responses were highly similar in the mirror neuron system (which is involved in mental simulation and understanding intentions), language comprehension areas, and the default-mode network, a group of regions activated when daydreaming, contemplating the future, observing the environment, or inferring others' intentions. There was little similarity in the neural responses between the two groups that held different interpretations of the story. The study concluded that "shared understanding elicits shared neural response."[58]

That conclusion is important. It's not just about a group hearing the same story, word for word. Instead, it's that they *shared a belief* about what that story meant. The same words are processed in the brain of the listener differently depending on what they believe. It means you can't just tell a story or deliver a message to your team and expect collective engagement and synchronized brains. Everyone comes with their own experiences, biases, and distractions that can get in the way of a common understanding. To synchronize, the group needs to make sense of what they're hearing in a similar way. How? In *Neuroscience for Learning and Development: How to Apply Neuroscience and Psychology for Improved Learning and Training*,[59] author Stella Collins offers advice similar to the conclusion of the Princeton study: Prime listeners' brains with the frame of reference you want them to use when they hear your message.

How to Prime Your Audience

In his book *Pre-suasion*,[60] social psychologist Dr. Robert Cialdini offers many ideas for priming your audience to be receptive to your message.

Timing. When are people most ready to hear and embrace something new? Think of when most diets, workout routines, and other significant changes are made: Mondays, the start of a new year, the first day of the month or season. Any time that feels like a "fresh start" is a good time to communicate a change.

Attention. Directly address your audience's current thoughts and feelings about your message (using second-person pronouns "you" and "your"), then steer their attention to the points you want to make. Cialdini says this approach harnesses the human tendency to ascribe unwarranted levels of importance to an idea as soon as one's attention is drawn to it.[61]

Association. Use words and images that are familiar to your audience, encouraging them to be open to your message. Make sure the associations these words and images trigger create positive thoughts and feelings about the concept(s) you want them to embrace.

How to Persuade Someone to Make a Change

What if the message you want to communicate involves persuading someone to make a difficult change? For most people, change is stressful, and this applies particularly to change in the workplace. A survey conducted by the American Psychological Association found that 55% of employees were stressed out at work due to changes in their workplaces.[62] Worse yet, people took the stress home with them, leading to drinking, drug use, and family problems. Understanding how to manage change through effective communication is more important than ever.

Research led by Emily Falk, an associate professor of communication, psychology, and marketing at the University of Pennsylvania's Annenberg School for Communication,[63] suggests that priming is important. This study focused on obese or overweight sedentary adults who were at risk for a range of health problems. Commonly, most messages about the need to be more active or eat healthier meals are met with defensiveness—the listener may agree with the premise but conclude that it doesn't apply to them.

To combat that natural self-defensive impulse, Falk and fellow researchers had half the participants engage in "self-transcendence tasks," which required them to think about things that mattered most to them (like family, friends, or spirituality) or to repeatedly wish for the well-being of people they knew and of strangers. They did these tasks while in an fMRI machine so researchers could see their brain activity in real time. The control group was tasked with thinking about the things that mattered least to them.

The researchers found that participants who engaged in self-transcendent thinking showed greater activity in brain areas involved in reward and positive valuation compared with the control group.

In the next step, all participants watched messages that either explained why their current lifestyle was negatively affecting their health or encouraged them to make explicit changes. For the next month, daily text messages reminded participants to think self-transcendent thoughts (or control thoughts) before they received the same kinds of health-conscious messages they saw in the lab. They also wore fitness trackers to monitor their activity. Amazingly, those who completed either of the self-transcendence tasks were significantly more active—not just right after the study but over the month that followed.

Falk and her fellow researchers even launched an app, Live Active!, that offers personalized daily messages, healthy choice "nudges," and an activity monitor to help people make and sustain difficult changes in their lives.

The lesson of this study is clear: Leaders should prime their teams to think about something bigger than themselves before delivering difficult news that will require people to change their behavior. This is as important for business leaders as it is for sports managers and even politicians.

First Impressions Matter

Remember the friend-or-foe response that happens almost immediately when we come into contact with someone? Whether you're beginning a one-on-one conversation, a speech to a large group, or something in between, first impressions matter. We know eye contact is key to connecting with others, but other nonverbal cues are also important.[64] Smiling and body positioning or posture can also influence whether your audience gets in sync with you.[65] If you already have a strong social connection, you're one step ahead.

In another study conducted by Princeton psychologist Uri Hasson,[66] participants were shown four different movie clips. The more compelling the content, the more the participants' brains synchronized. The most compelling was a tense bank robbery scene from *Dog Day Afternoon*, and the least was a clip made by pointing a camera at a crowd of people watching a concert in a New York City park.

Research by Sam Barnett and Moran Cerf at Northwestern's Kellogg School of Management takes Hasson's work a step further. They found that higher levels of engagement and brain synchrony in a small focus group of viewers watching movie trailers correlated surprisingly well with subsequent movie ticket sales across the entire United States.[67] Their takeaway? The simplest trailers with the fewest words and cleanest visuals achieved higher engagement and future ticket sales. They were simply more persuasive.

These findings give us some general guidelines for communication that engages with and even encourages action from our audience. So the question now is, What, exactly, is compelling? What's simple? And how can we translate the data into action?

Neuroscientists are providing some new answers to these questions.

Keep It Simple

When you're trying to maximize engagement with your verbal communication, keep in mind that neural similarity is hindered by complexity.[68] In other words, keep it simple!

That's what Barnett and Cerf found out in a darkened movie theater. The most effective trailers, in terms of creating brain synchrony and driving ticket sales, had the fewest spoken words and the fewest faces and other stimuli on the screen. The best was a trailer for *X-Men: Days of Future Past*. It had the highest synchrony score, was remembered by the majority of viewers in the study, and performed the best at the global box office of all the movies studied. It was also a very simple trailer, typically showing one face on the screen at a time with only one person speaking. The worst was the trailer for *Mr. Peabody and Sherman*, which had half a dozen characters running around and talking at the same time. It had the lowest synchrony score, and its global box office take was less than a quarter of what *X-Men* earned. While other factors, such as familiarity with the X-Men franchise and target audience (in the case of Mr. Peabody, children), no doubt contributed to box office performance, the general principle held up across the trailers in the study. Simpler trailers triggered higher brain synchrony across viewers, which predicted better ticket sales. The simpler the message, the easier it is to understand, and ultimately the more likely it will be to be remembered.

Simplicity

In the book *Made to Stick*,[69] researchers Chip and Dan Heath come to a similar conclusion. They offer six principles for making your ideas understood and remembered, and the first is simplicity. But, they argue, it's not just "short and sweet." The Heaths say it's about communicating an essential core, something that's both simple and profound.

Multisensory Language

Another tool is using "multisensory" language to help people imagine and even feel as though they're experiencing what you're describing. Neuroscientists at Emory University revealed that metaphors that include textural imagery activate the same region of the brain in listeners that would have been activated if they were actually sensing texture through touch.[70] A study in Spain showed that reading words associated with smells (think lavender, cinnamon, and garlic) activates the brain's olfactory regions.[71] By stimulating more of the sensory cortex through this type of language, you're creating a richer type of engagement.

Driving People to Action

Wharton marketing professor Jonah Berger makes another recommendation in his book *Contagious: Why Things Catch On*. Research shows that when you choose a "high arousal" emotion to link to your message, such as awe, excitement, or humor, you create higher levels of engagement. "Emotions drive people to action," he writes. "So rather than quoting statistics or providing information, we need to focus on feelings."[72] Couple this with evidence from another Wharton study on work motivation: Professor Adam Grant found that when employees discover how their work has a positive impact on others, they're both happier and more productive.[73] Tell an inspirational story about how your team or organization is making a difference, and you'll resonate with your audience on a number of levels. As we saw with Emily Falk's work on self-transcendence, this will also make listeners more likely to hear your message and do the hard work to make a change.

SPEAK UP!

Berger and Alex Van Zant of Rutgers Business School have also examined how the way we speak affects our persuasiveness.[74] One of their conclusions is that speaking slightly louder than normal, and varying your overall volume, increases the perception of your confidence, which in turn makes you more persuasive. Of course, that only works when you're physically present, which ties in with another finding: You're more persuasive in person than in an email.

"There's work that shows people seem more human when we hear their voice. We give them more sense of mind, we think of them more as real people when they use their voice. Our research also suggests it can make people more persuasive," writes Berger.[75]

Talk About the Now

A linguistic analysis of hundreds of visionary leaders also provides some guidance on fine-tuning your message.[76] In addition to keeping it simple and using "perceptual" language, the analysis found that talking about the present (rather than the future) and using second-person pronouns (directly addressing the audience) were highly effective. Noah Zandan, the cofounder of Quantified Communications, which studies and gathered research on how the visionary leaders communicated, offered an example: "If you think about Elon Musk talking about Tesla, he always talks about what it's like to drive in the car, what it's like to look at the car, how the doors work. It's really less about the future of energy and transport. As this kind of theoretical vehicle, he really brings it and makes it tangible." Present tense, he said, is "highly correlated with credibility. . . . People think if you're talking so much about the future, then it's going to be less credible."

Giving Feedback That Actually Leads to Results

At a basic level, humans (as well as many other organisms) rely on feedback for survival. We learn from cues in our environment ("it looks like a predator is near," "we'll find better food over there") to positively adjust and adapt our behaviors. In the workplace, feedback is a critical part of development and achievement. When we learn the kinds of skills and knowledge we need to progress, and how to obtain them, we can improve our performance.

According to a number of studies, including LinkedIn's 2018 Workforce Learning Report,[77] a large majority of employees (LinkedIn says 93%) expect career-development opportunities from their employers. But not enough managers are delivering, and, according to Wharton management professor Peter Cappelli, the ones that do get it all wrong.[78]

Annual performance reviews, key performance indicators, and 360-degree feedback assessments have been under fire for decades. Two other popular approaches, the sandwich or hamburger model and "start, stop, continue" (in which an employee is encouraged to start a new behavior, stop a current one, and continue a third), have also been debunked,[79] but many companies still use them. Others have taken elements of these approaches to extremes. The *Wall Street Journal* described the "radical candor" of the "Netflix way"—a culture that current and former employees said was, at its worst, "ruthless, demoralizing and transparent to the point of dysfunctional."[80]

Encourage Your Employees to Ask for Feedback

So how can managers deliver the feedback that employees want in a way that actually improves performance—and doesn't destroy morale and company culture in the process? To start, let's go back to what we know about the social brain network and how to engage with the person you're speaking to. Eye contact and mirroring (see earlier in chapters 2 and 3) are critical for initiating brain synchrony, which means you have primed the employee to really hear what you have to say. Then, it's all about what you say and when and how you say it.

A study led by Tessa West and Katherine Thorson of New York University's NeuroLeadership Institute used heart-rate monitors on subjects while they were engaged in giving or receiving unprompted feedback.[81] After engaging in a mock negotiation, half the participants were told to give unprompted feedback, and the other half were instructed to ask for feedback. Perhaps not surprisingly, anxiety levels rose for both the giver and the receiver (although receivers' heart rates jumped higher) during the feedback. It seems that as much as we don't like hearing it, we don't like delivering it either.

But the study offered an even more interesting insight. When the researchers asked each group how they felt during the feedback, they found that although the participants were uncomfortable asking for feedback, doing so helped equip them to hear and process it. Their innate "threat response" was lower. In fact, granting permission "is hugely important for putting both parties in a psychological state that's ready for negative news. Without it, the brain begins to revert to a state that isn't conducive to growth, and that finds its roots thousands of years in the past."[82]

So encouraging your direct reports to ask for feedback instead of offering it unprompted works much better. You might suggest that when they get a generally positive reaction, such as "good job," they ask for more specifics ("In what way?" "What in particular did you think I did well?").

Negative Feedback Is All About Being Specific

Remember Google's Project Oxygen and its end product, "Eight Habits of Highly Effective Managers"? The first habit is to be a good coach, which means, in part, to "have regular one-on-ones, presenting solutions to problems tailored to the employee's strengths."[83] It also means providing "specific, constructive feedback, balancing negative and positive." But if we prefer positive feedback, building on strengths, how and when do you give negative feedback?

Even when it's needed, negative feedback can be ignored or dismissed, because it can trigger the fight-or-flight sympathetic nervous system. This survival mechanism evolved to help us deal with threats—real or perceived. Once it's triggered, epinephrine (also known as adrenaline) is released into the bloodstream, causing a burst of energy that makes the heart beat faster and breathing quicken. Someone in this mode isn't exactly receptive to learning.

Giving negative feedback that motivates change, then, requires that you work to reduce or even eliminate the fight-or-flight response. Need to send an email to schedule the discussion? Avoid mentioning that there are some important "issues" that need to be addressed. Sounding vaguely threatening a day or two ahead will make it nearly impossible for your message to sink in. It's better to meet face-to-face and hold their gaze. Mutual eye contact improves retention of what's been said, and makes people more self-aware.[84]

Another idea is to first schedule a meeting during which the employee evaluates you and how well you are supporting him or her in their development and current role. It's vital that you listen uncritically, take your time responding, and even use mirroring by repeating the feedback in your own words. ("Let me make sure I understand what you said.")

When you hold the second meeting, in which you will deliver some potentially hard-to-hear feedback to the employee, go back to what you heard in the first meeting. Ask how you can help support the growth or change you are seeking. If that was an area of perceived weakness, ask for specific ways you might improve.

How to Address a Negative

So far we've talked about engagement with positive, or at least neutral, messages. But what if you have to communicate or address bad news? Hint: Don't cite statistics or blame the victim, as Musk did after Tesla owner Walter Huang died when the autopilot steered the car into a cement barrier.[85]

First, don't ignore it. Research at Columbia University shows that suppressing negative emotions doesn't work.[86] Even when people believed they looked as though nothing was wrong, their limbic system (the brain's emotion center) was just as aroused as without suppression, and in some cases it was even more aroused. This approach was used effectively by New York governor Andrew Cuomo in his daily press briefings during the COVID-19 pandemic. Cuomo was widely praised for being honest and up front with his emotions.

Second, label the emotion. A UCLA study, "Putting Feelings into Words,"[87] found that as participants looked at pictures of people with emotional expressions, their amygdalas activated. But when they were asked to name the emotion, that impact was lessened: The ventrolateral prefrontal cortex activated and the emotional amygdala reactivity was reduced. Again, Cuomo effectively reduced his constituents' natural fear by openly talking about the coronavirus. German chancellor Angela Merkel also used this strategy to help the German people understand why they needed to practice difficult social distancing measures to slow the spread of the coronavirus.

The Leader's Brainwaves: Things to Remember

- Use storytelling to get a group to embrace an idea, and prime people's brains to be more receptive to that idea.
- Modulate your volume, focus on the present, and directly address your audience to increase the perception of confidence and trust in your ideas.
- If you need to communicate a difficult message, prime your audience to think about something bigger than themselves— their team, community, or nation—to overcome their default resistance. They will be more likely to really "hear" your message and do the hard work needed to get the job done.
- Make feedback a two-way street. Ask your team members to evaluate you, and encourage them to ask you to evaluate them. Don't be vague: Specify what needs to be improved on and offer a clear path forward.

Chapter 4

Harnessing the Brain's "Innovation Engine"
How to Drive Creative Thinking

If you could, would you take a pill to make you more creative, resilient, energetic, and able to improve multitasking, risk-taking, and crisis management? What if its side effects included procrastination, disorganization, forgetfulness, inability to concentrate, and distractibility? Still interested? For those diagnosed with attention-deficit/hyperactivity disorder, better known as ADHD, the only choice is to live with all these traits (and learn to manage the downsides) or treat them with medication.

Super-successful entrepreneurs such as JetBlue founder David Neeleman and Spartan CEO Joe De Sena credit their ADHD, and specifically the hyperfocus and creative problem solving that come with it, for their achievements.[88] Famous leaders such as Microsoft cofounder Bill Gates, Virgin Group founder Richard Branson, Ikea founder Ingvar Kamprad, Cisco Systems CEO John T. Chambers, and Charles Schwab also have been open about being diagnosed with ADHD.

Many of these business leaders have created corporate cultures that embrace the creativity that comes so naturally to them. Not only are they more innovative with stronger brand recognition,[89] but they're actually more fun to work for. A study by Adobe and Forrester Consulting also revealed that creativity impacts growth and market share: Creative companies' revenue growth dramatically outpaces that of their peers, and they also outpace competitors in market share and market leadership positions.[90]

It's clear that creativity is crucial for business success. It's also clear that it's in short supply: 61% of companies in the Adobe study reported that they are not creative. (The study quotes Harvard professor Teresa Amabile, who says "creativity is the production of novel and useful ideas in any domain.")

The good news from neuroscientists is that they've discovered where creativity resides in the brain—and how to access it. And while some people are clearly born with more creativity than others, we now know that everyone can turn up their creativity dial to reach their full innovation potential.

Left Brain/Right Brain Is a Myth

When you consider creativity and the brain, your first thought might be the right brain/left brain theory. In "right brain" people, the theory goes, the right side of the brain is dominant, and it's responsible for creative, divergent thinking. "Left brain" people, with the left side of the brain dominant, are more logical and analytical.

Despite a number of studies that have debunked this as myth, including one at the University of Utah led by professor of neuroradiology Jeff Anderson,[91] it persists. What new research shows instead is that there is indeed an "innovation circuit" that supports exploration, divergent thinking, and creativity.[92] But this circuit lives in both sides of the brain.

The heart of the brain's innovation engine is the default-mode network, so called because it was discovered when scientists were scanning people's brains while they took breaks between tasks.[93] About 20 years ago, neurologists collected brain data from participants while they were performing a task and also when they were idle. The scientists discovered that during the time between task performances, a specific set of brain areas was active. Whenever people were allowed to relax and let their minds wander, this area was strongly activated; but when they went back to performing simple routine tasks, the default network shut off. And in fact, people who report more mind wandering during the day show stronger baseline activity in this network than people who day-dream less. It seems to play an important role in exploration, spinning out new ideas, and even imagining the future.

There's also an opposing circuit that supports focus and routine task performance, sometimes called the "frontoparietal attention network," which just means it lives in the front and sides of your brain. This circuit is most active when you are concentrating on a single task, especially rote ones like doing arithmetic or pushing buttons in response to prompts.

One of the fascinating things about these circuits is that when one is turned up, the other is turned down. That means if you're working on some routine task like data entry in an Excel spreadsheet or answering email, it's pretty hard to be dreaming up new product innovations.

Exploration is important for almost all animals, as you'll see in a bit. And in fact, monkeys have these same networks for exploration and focus too. We found that neurons in monkeys' innovation engines fired tens of seconds before they made the decision to try a new option or diverge from a habitual routine.[94] Even more importantly, when we stimulated these neurons electrically, monkeys actively tried something new.[95] When we shut these neurons off, monkeys couldn't learn new patterns, because they stuck to their old routines.[96] This is important evidence that activity levels in the brain's innovation network actually do drive exploration and divergent thinking.

Testing Your Creative Potential

Ready to see how robust your innovation network is? Take this simple test: Grab a piece of paper and a pen and set a timer for 90 seconds. Ready? Write down as many alternative uses as you can think of for a brick—the crazier the better.

I've had executives and MBA students in my classroom who often come up with 10 or more uses (did you come up with a weapon, birdfeeder, or trivet?). The Alternative Uses Test was designed by J. P. Guilford in 1967 as a means to evaluate divergent thinking ability, or what Guilford called "spontaneous flexibility."[97]

The Alternative Uses Test is an interesting exercise, but in terms of neuroscience, it goes beyond the wild ideas that are generated. Remember the innovation and focus/rote task circuits? While you were thinking up alternative uses, the innovation circuit in your brain was revved up, and the task circuit was suppressed. Understanding how that works—and especially how we can access and stimulate the former—is key to managing creativity and innovation.

Should I Stay or Should I Go?

Your ability to come up with alternative uses, and the need for that ability to explore new opportunities and ideas, is built into the brain. Not just human brains though. Mice, insects, and invertebrates all have it too. This fundamental ability is tied to the act of *foraging* and the choice that lies at the heart of the question made famous by the punk rock band the Clash: "Should I stay or should I go?"

Here's one way to look at it: When an animal is looking for and consuming food in one place, there's a cost for staying there. While it is risky and potentially time-consuming, moving to another spot may yield more or better food. This choice looks the same in your brain whether you're deciding to keep fishing in the same pond, move to a different company or accept a new role within the same company, or continue to look for that perfect lamp on a website.[98] All these decisions are about *opportunity cost*—managing the trade-off of sticking with what you know versus searching for something new. All animals have to make these decisions, and many of them use the same brain circuit we do. Remarkably, all animals, including humans, appear to use the same algorithm to make this decision, even when this computation is implemented in radically different kinds of brains.

To understand how our brains manage this trade-off, we need to look at ecologist Eric Charnov's Marginal Value Theorem of Optimal Foraging.[99] Charnov sought to provide a mathematical answer to the question of what's behind an individual's decision to leave one patch and search for another. Charnov developed this theory when he was a PhD student at the University of Michigan, and it's now one of the most highly cited papers in all of theoretical biology. His theory identifies the optimal decision between two extremes: spending too much time in a patch with declining resources or spending too much time searching for a new patch.

In Charnov's model, the richness of the environment is a key variable for making this trade-off. Imagine you make your living by picking apples. If there is only one apple tree for miles, you should stay put and harvest all the apples in the nearest tree. But if you're in an orchard full of apple trees, you should move from tree to tree picking the apples that are easiest to reach. Hundreds of different animals have been tested in labs and in the wild, and all forage as predicted by the Marginal Value Theorem. That includes humans too—whether hunting for seals in the Arctic, shopping for groceries at Whole Foods, or surfing the internet.

The Roots of Creativity

What does all this have to do with creativity? It turns out that foraging is at the root of exploration and innovation. The brain has a foraging circuit (and our lab was one of the first to locate it).[100] Remember the discovery of the brain's "innovation circuit" while a researcher was collecting brain data from study participants when they were idle? This circuit overlaps with the foraging circuit, and it is made up of two key areas:

- The *anterior cingulate cortex* helps you figure out the value of moving on to another patch (or store aisle, or website, or job). Its activity peaks right before you move on.

- The *posterior cingulate cortex*, the hub of the brain's innovation engine, calculates more strategically over a longer period of time whether you are in a rich or poor environment. When it is activated, it promotes exploration and divergent thinking.

These two areas are heavily connected, and they are involved in regulating whether you are in an exploratory or focused state.

Neuroscientists have also studied the genetics of foraging using the roundworm *Caenorhabditis elegans* (typically referred to as *C. elegans*).[101] It's perfect for this research because it is transparent and has only 302 neurons, and scientists know a lot about what each one does. These worms are also easy to maintain in the lab because they are very good at sitting in a petri dish and sucking up all the bacteria surrounding them. In other words, the worms studied in the lab are genetically predisposed to be focused and tend to fully exploit the closest resources.

About nine years ago, scientists discovered a different type of roundworm in Hawaii that behaves in the opposite way—it's the Steve Jobs of worms, a consummate explorer. Its nervous system has a lower threshold for exploration genetically encoded in it.[102] The difference in behavior between typical lab worms and the Hawaiian worms is rooted in receptors for two important chemicals: dopamine, which is tied to habit formation and reinforcement learning, and norepinephrine, which plays a role in the change states that let you break your habits. Both are related to the trade-off between exploring and exploiting.

In humans, we can get a measure of the levels of these chemicals noninvasively by pointing a camera at your eyes and estimate where you are in terms of exploration and exploitation. The size of your pupil dynamically indexes norepinephrine levels. A wider pupil signifies more of the chemical, which means greater readiness to explore.[103] Pupil size can therefore be used as a biomarker for your creative state, and your average pupil size also tells us something about how creative you are compared with someone else.

A recent study linked blink rate to dopamine levels.[104] The more you naturally blink, the more dopamine is being released in your brain. Unfortunately, this can't be reversed: Conscious rapid blinking won't release more dopamine.

How to Spark Creativity

I've already mentioned that we're all born, like Hawaiian roundworms, with an innate ability to explore. But that ability can be "dialed up" relatively easily. To do that, though, we need to assess our baseline. In addition to using assessments like the Alternative Uses Test, researchers have used anagrams, a simple game that involves randomly choosing a number of alphabet tiles and making as many words from those tiles as possible. When a player believes they can't make any more words (just as an animal foraging for food believes a particular patch will no longer yield anything worthwhile), the player can swap the remaining tiles for randomly chosen new ones. It's the word-game version of "should I stay or should I go."

It turns out there's a baseline for individuals in terms of when they typically "forage" for new tiles, but scientists have figured out that it can be manipulated. In one study, participants played an online game that involved collecting resources by clicking on them with a cursor before they played anagrams.[105] One group of participants discovered that resources were clumped together—they didn't have to move the cursor far to collect them. A second group encountered resources that were more spread out, forcing them to search more widely. Then both groups moved on to anagrams. Participants who were in the first group for the online game took much longer to dump their letters than participants in the second group. They were, in other words, primed to exploit rather than explore. The carryover effect is remarkable: Playing the online foraging game put participants' brains in a different state—at least for a short period of time.

Turning Up Your Innovation Dial

You don't have to play a foraging game to optimize your brain for creativity. There are a few simple things you can do instead to activate the exploration network. Remember, your brain can't fully access the innovation circuit and the task circuit at the same time. That means the first thing you need to do to boost creativity is to deliberately turn off your analytical mind. By separating yourself from routine tasks like answering emails, working on a spreadsheet, or handling payroll or time sheets, you give your brain the chance to fire up the innovation circuit.

Walk This Way

One way to achieve that separation is by walking. LinkedIn CEO Jeff Weiner, like Aristotle, Freud, Truman, Darwin, and Beethoven before him, encourages walking as part of the workday.[106] A study at Stanford found that creative output increased by an average of 60% when walking, compared with sitting.[107] It also found that indoor walks were just as effective as outdoor walks and that the benefits were realized after walks of just 5–16 minutes.

Walking isn't the only way to "step away" from analytical tasks. Because the brain is often at its most creative when it's not working on a specific problem, people tend to have their best new ideas when engaged in "mindless" tasks. When you need a fresh approach to an issue, try focusing on it briefly to clearly define the situation, then put it aside. Your subconscious mind—which is often the source of novel ideas—will continue to work on the task while you engage in mundane activities like driving or folding laundry, or even overnight as you sleep. New solutions can naturally bubble up to consciousness after this form of "creative procrastination."[108]

Walk It Out

Don't take my word (or Darwin's or Beethoven's) for the benefits of walking. To see the effect that walking can have on your creative state, try performing another Alternative Uses Test (find one online at www.creativehuddle.co.uk). First, take a regular test. Then, take a 10-minute walk, followed by another test. You should notice improved performance on the second test.

Get Social

Socializing also boosts activity in the brain's exploration system. Many companies encourage it as a means to ramp up creativity. At IDEO, it's over a meal (think soup on Fridays, tea and cookies on Tuesday). For Virgin Atlantic, it's on outings to sporting and other events. London-based public relations agency PHA Media lets its employees make the call: It provides a quarterly budget for activities of the staff's choosing, such as playing paintball and attending the theater.[109] You can use this insight personally too: When you're taking a much-needed break, socialize with a colleague.

Dial Down Stress

Research also shows that stress blocks the exploration and creativity system. Practices like meditation, known to reduce stress, are credited by a growing number of business leaders as an integral tool for creativity. Salesforce CEO Marc Benioff says meditation allows him to take a step back, clear his mind, and make room for new ideas—a state he calls "beginner's mind."[110] Former tech entrepreneur Charly Kleissner says his meditation practice allowed him to cofound the 100% IMPACT Network, joining with other investors in a commitment to invest 100% of their assets for social and/or environmental impact.[111]

Fostering Team Creativity

So far we've learned that everyone is born with an innovation/exploration circuit that's set at a specific level, and that it can be "dialed up" by performing simple exercises. We also know that businesses need innovative thinkers in order to thrive and that they're in short supply. But can we go further? Research suggests we can.[112]

From design-thinking workshops to innovation tournaments, organizations are investing significant amounts in programs that promise to nurture creativity. David Tanner, former director of the DuPont Center for Creativity and Innovation, says the company used a lateral-thinking creativity tool to pursue original ideas for cost reduction. It saved DuPont more than $5 million over 10 years.[113]

Recognizing that economic rewards don't necessarily spark creativity or build a creative culture, Australian software company Atlassian holds four "ShipIt" days a year. Employees set aside their regular work and have 24 hours to work on the creative project of their choice. ShipIt days have resulted in product fixes, a DIY video studio for creating content for the company's blog and website, a miniarcade—and a happier, more engaged workforce.[114] Dozens of companies, including Google, now embrace similar practices.

Creativity training can also improve innovative thinking in people whose dials are already set high. In one fascinating study at the University of Western Ontario,[115] Joel Lopata looked at pianists' brainwaves while they either listened to, played back, or improvised jazz melodies. Some of the participants had prior training in improvisation, while others did not.

Lopata found that alpha brainwaves, which go down when we focus on something outside our own minds, increased in the trained musicians when they were improvising. This didn't happen with the untrained pianists.

"What we found was a distinct pattern of activity in the front right brain area, which suggests that while these musicians were improvising creatively, they were in what we call 'a creative mental state,'" he said. "They were in a distinct state of consciousness different from when they are thinking more rationally and logically."

Remember your experience with the Alternative Uses Test, when your innovation circuit was firing and your rote task circuit was suppressed? That's what happened with the pianists who were trained in improvisation.

"There are two different modes (in the brain) and we only observed that (creative mode) in individuals that had previous training in improvisation—not in those that didn't have that training," Lopata said. "That suggests that that creative mental state is something that is likely best learned through formal training."[116]

Matching Brains to the Right Jobs

I noted at the beginning of this chapter that some people are born with a stronger innovation circuit. In fact, scientists have found that genetics contributes strongly to developing the circuitry for exploration, and these genes are commonly found in writers, painters, musicians, and entrepreneurs. There is also a strong overlap of that circuitry and the genes involved in schizophrenia, bipolar disorder, and attention deficit disorder (ADD)/ADHD.[117]

About 15 years ago, a team of anthropologists and geneticists studied the Ariaal, a group of pastoral nomads who live in Kenya.[118] These subsistence hunter-gatherers have a high rate of a gene mutation for ADHD (extreme exploration): about one-fifth of them had it, compared with less than 10% in US schoolchildren.[119] The study took place after about half the Ariaal tribe moved to villages and took up a more sedentary life that included very repetitive work. Researchers found that nomads who had the ADHD-linked mutation and spent their days roaming the savannah while herding cattle, camels, and goats were relatively well nourished and healthy. But the health of the settled tribe members' with the ADHD mutation was deteriorating.

This study shows the dramatic effect of mismatching innate talents with tasks. For those predisposed to explore, a role that rewards it (such as art director or web designer) makes much more sense. In the United States, we tend to medicate people, especially kids, who are naturally fidgety and primed to explore, by giving them Ritalin or Adderall to make it easier to sit still and focus. Likewise, promoting someone who naturally tends to be less exploratory to run a design lab probably won't yield good results for the organization or the employee.

Alphabet, the umbrella company of Google, has begun managing differences in creativity by putting people in jobs that suit them. Judging by the change in corporate culture, it seems that natural innovators work for GoogleX—where "moonshot" projects are dreamed up—while the natural doers keep Google Search, Gmail, and Google Calendar humming. Because most organizations have a range of positions for innovation explorers and more task-oriented abilities, it makes good business sense for management to align talent with jobs. In other words, instead of trying to make people conform to a specific job role, match their natural talents for innovation or task completion to the job at hand. People with ADHD may be genetically well suited to a hunter-gatherer life, but that doesn't mean their innate skills can't be put to good use in more creative, albeit "conventional," careers. And people who crave routine are unlikely to thrive in jobs requiring constant innovation.

These findings also have a more personal application. At different times of the day, you may be more inclined to either think more creatively or tackle focused tasks like filling out a time sheet or answering email. That's the premise of Daniel Pink's latest book, *When: The Scientific Secrets of Perfect Timing.*[120] Pink says most people (night owls are the exception) are best able to make good decisions in the mid to late morning rather than in the afternoon, when we become sluggish. But then we recover—and that's the time when it makes sense to work on more creative projects, and to socialize, which can be an important component in brainstorming.

Why not time your activities to match these brain states? Think of the kinds of tasks you need to accomplish, and which of those tasks require you to be in focused, exploit mode and which would benefit from explore mode. It's a sound neuroscience-based approach to productivity that takes advantage of your strengths throughout the day. Soon, we may even be able to do this scientifically by using data from a micro-EEG or even measurements of pupil size through the camera on your computer.

The Leader's Brainwaves: Things to Remember

- Everyone has an innovation circuit in their brain, but it's not the left brain/right brain system commonly portrayed in popular media. This circuit activates when we explore but shuts down when we perform rote tasks.
- You can spark more innovative thinking for yourself, and nurture it in others, by building in breaks from routine work. Put away the spreadsheet and go for a walk or chat with a friend to rev up your brain's innovation network.
- There really are more creative people and more task-oriented people. We can use that knowledge to better match people to jobs. They will perform better and be happier too.
- When you need to find creative solutions, rev up your employees' innovation engines by priming them with foraging games or pushing them out of their comfort zones. This will make them a little more ready to explore new options and engage in divergent thinking.

Chapter 5

Decision-Making 101
The Five-Step Process and
How to Get It Right

They're painful, legendary tales of decisions that haunt the leaders who made them. Billionaire founder of Electronic Data Systems Ross Perot could have bought Microsoft in 1979 for $40 million to $60 million. Kodak invented the digital camera and filed for bankruptcy by not embracing it quickly enough. The AOL–Time Warner merger, arguably the worst in history, lost about $100 billion in stock value. Blockbuster CEO John Antioco turned down an offer to join forces with Netflix for $50 million. And remember the GE-Alstom deal from chapter 2?

These decisions—and others like them—routinely make "worst ever" lists, but there isn't as much written about the why (other than blaming arrogance and overconfidence). It's too late for people like Perot, Antioco, and Immelt, but neuroscience is providing new insights into how we make decisions, where we can go wrong, and how to stay on track.

In the late 1990s, I was among a small group of neuroscientists and economists that tried to reconcile different ideas about decision-making by directly studying the neurobiology behind decisions. Seminal work in this new field—sometimes called "neuroeconomics" or "decision neuroscience"—discovered the brain uses an elegant and mathematically optimal algorithm to make decisions, which considers both the evidence supporting a decision and its value to us. It turns out that some, and perhaps many, so-called irrationalities arise from physiological constraints or imperfections and variations in the underlying mechanism, as we'll see.

In this chapter, we will look at how the basic decision-making process works and how it varies across people. We will also examine how our brain physiology limits the number of options we can usefully consider. The implications of both for leaders will be explored. We'll also look at the famous (at least among neuroscientists) "jam jar" study that illustrates the paradox of choice (give people too many options and they'll opt to choose nothing). While it's being constantly debated, the original conclusion—limiting options leads to increased sales—can now be supported by neuroscience findings about brain physiology.

The Five-Step Process

When you make a decision, your brain goes through five sequential steps:

1. *Sense your options.* This is the point at which you realize a decision should be made. You're sensing something about yourself ("I'm hungry") or your environment ("There's a doughnut and an apple on the tray in front of me").
2. *Weigh the evidence.* This is where you consider your options ("Is the apple ripe or rotten?" "Is the doughnut glazed or chocolate?").
3. *Consider the value of the options.* At this point, you take into account the expected outcomes of selecting each of the available options ("Ripe apples taste better than rotten apples," "Eating too many doughnuts makes you gain weight").
4. *Make a choice and take action.* ("Eat the doughnut"—you know you want to).
5. *Evaluate the outcome.* What were the consequences of your decision? Did it resolve the issue you identified in step 1? Would you make the same decision again if circumstances

were similar? ("I ate the doughnut and it tasted great—but now I feel fat").

People often ask me the location of the brain's decision-making area. The truth is that the whole brain is involved in making decisions. While you (or a monkey, or a mouse) are working your way through a decision, the whole brain is devoted to gathering evidence, weighing the options, making a choice, and learning from the outcome.

Why You Can't Be Fast and Accurate at the Same Time

Under optimal conditions, you can weigh the evidence plus what you value to make a straightforward decision relatively quickly. But what if the decision is more complex? It could be more important, have more options, or involve other people. What if the complexity involves a dynamic flow of information, like choosing to hold on to, sell, or buy stock? Think of this situation like a traffic light on a foggy night: You might make an error just because the signal isn't clear. In this kind of environment, you may want to set a higher threshold for making a decision by collecting more information and taking more time to consider your options. Unfortunately, being accurate typically means being slower. In the extreme, you're like Hamlet—unable to make a decision.

When the decision is complex and you don't have the luxury of slowing down, you have no choice but to make a trade-off between speed and accuracy. For example, a soldier on night patrol who sees someone walking toward her with an arm raised has very little time to decide whether he's holding a cell phone, a weapon, or something else. There's a high degree of urgency, and it's easy to arrive at the wrong decision because there's both a slow accumulation of information and the environment is not optimal (it's dark and there's too much distance to see clearly).

Improving Decisions with Meditation

Research conducted at INSEAD and the Wharton School, and published in the journal *Psychological Science*, found that even quick, short-term mindfulness meditative practice can help you make better decisions.[121] Specifically, the study found that meditation can help counteract the tendency to continue to spend resources on something that doesn't warrant it in an attempt to recover an original investment or to break even. Commonly known as "throwing good money after bad," sunk-cost bias is recognized as one of the most common and costly destructive cognitive biases affecting organizations today. It causes leaders to base decisions on past behavior and a desire not to waste resources already spent, instead of cutting their losses and choosing a new option that would lead to the best outcome.

Short periods of meditation help develop resistance to this flawed decision process and encourage people to make more rational decisions by considering more of the information available in the present moment. By reducing focus on the past and future, meditation causes a psychological shift that leads to less negative emotion. The reduced negative emotion then facilitates the decision to let go of "sunk costs," leading to a better perspective and smarter decision-making.

In the end, we're often faced with deciding, before we decide, whether it's more important to be correct or fast. Weighing the evidence and evaluating your options takes time, and that process is wired into the way our brains make decisions. Whenever you can, slow down to make better decisions. If the decision must be made rapidly, be prepared to tolerate mistakes and make contingency plans just in case.

What We See and Where We Look Affect What We Choose

Next time you are in a meeting, either in person or online, pay careful attention to where you are looking. You might find yourself looking from person to person around the table or in the tiny "Hollywood Squares" boxes on Zoom. Your gaze might flit back to someone you've already scanned when they start to speak, and then dart to the PowerPoint slide deck on-screen as they begin describing new earnings forecasts. What you didn't see, thanks to your brain, was everything in this scene upside down, as a series of separate blurry images, or one blurry image with a clear view at the center of your gaze. But that's the way your eyes take it in.

We actually see very clearly—for only about the width of our thumb held out at arm's length. We move our eyes about four times per second, and when they are in flight we are actually blind. But our brains reassemble the stop and start, clear middle and blurry background, snapshots into the single coherent, focused picture we perceive.

Neuroscientists have studied eye movements extensively using various tracking devices. What they've found are characteristic patterns of looking at things. Faces in particular attract our attention, and we tend to first look at each eye, and then the mouth, in a triangular pattern.[122] But different people's brains prioritize different information. For example, people with autism tend not to look at others' faces, while those with certain forms of anxiety avoid making eye contact.

The information you are seeking also shapes where you look. In one of the very first eye-tracking studies, Alfred Yarbus showed people a painting of a family at their dining-room table and asked them to guess the family's wealth.[123] Instead of focusing first on faces, they looked at details like clothing, how the room was decorated, and the fact that a servant was present. We use our eyes to sample information differently depending on the decision we need to make.

In the past decade, eye-tracking studies have revealed the ways in which webpage design powerfully shapes where people look— and what they subsequently remember and buy.[124] People in Western societies, who are accustomed to reading from left to write, tend to scan web pages in an "F"-shaped pattern, beginning at the upper left and moving rightward and downward.[125] Web designers can either adapt to that pattern or use prominent visuals, arrows, and other attention-grabbing elements to break that pattern. Perhaps most importantly, the fact that our gaze is instinctively drawn to faces can be used to attract and hold the attention of people browsing a website. These same principles apply to retail environments and the office but are much easier to control online, thus offering more opportunity to shape attention while people are working, and shopping, remotely.

What's happening in our brains when we look around the conference table, scan a grocery shelf, or use videoconferencing apps to meet online? Neuroscientists have discovered that there is a "priority map" for what we see in the brain.[126] We now know that we are quicker to respond to a visual stimulus when it is expected, and we pay more attention to people and objects that stand out. These types of attention happen at the expense of the rest of the visual scene, which gets muted. The brain's priority map basically boosts the "volume" on visual stimuli that pop out from the background or that we value more.

Why is it important to understand what we're looking at and therefore paying attention to? Neuroscience has identified a direct relationship between what we look at and what we choose. As you contemplate a decision, your brain conducts a sampling process that weighs up information about your options. But it doesn't necessarily do this in a balanced way, seeking information about every choice equally. The more you pay attention to one option, the less aware you are of the qualities of other options. We often are not even aware of things that we are not actively paying attention to. We filter out a lot of information in order to consciously take in an object, behavior, or idea (like Immelt and the Alstom deal). That's one reason manufacturers want their products placed at eye level in stores. In other words, where you look and how much attention you pay affect your choices.

Scientists watching which option you're looking at and for how long can actually predict your ultimate choice. How much attention we pay to any option also can be manipulated by changing what it looks like. When our attention is manipulated in this way, we are more likely to choose the most visible or otherwise conspicuous option and will often report liking that option more—a process known as the "mere exposure effect." By changing key aspects of an option to make it stand out more (brighter colors, higher contrast, use of faces), you can subtly shape the decision someone makes.

Here's a good example. Most people are loss averse, demanding more potential gain than loss to accept a gamble.[127] This is one reason most people buy insurance: They will pay money to avoid a potential loss. In a recent study, we found that the level of loss-aversion in individuals is betrayed by where they look.[128] People were given a choice to accept or reject a gamble offering equal odds of winning and losing money. The amount of gain and loss offered varied from trial to trial. Our participants were generally loss averse, but some were not. We found that people who spent more time looking at the potential loss were more likely to reject gambles—even when they were favorable. Another study, by Cary Frydman and Antonio Rangel,[129] found that people were more likely to hold on to losing stocks when their prices were made more salient. In ongoing work, we're finding that merely presenting potential gains in a slightly brighter or larger font can actually erase loss aversion. These findings demonstrate a tight link between the way financial information is presented visually and what people choose.

These findings extend to consumer decision-making as well. When snack-food packages are bright or colorful, people are more likely to look at them. And the more they look at them, the likelier they are to choose them—even when they're not their preferred snack foods.[130]

So, where we look introduces bias into the way our brains evaluate our options. And that means that if we can get people to look longer or first at something, we can nudge them toward choosing it. This can be powerful not only as a marketing tool but also in helping to improve health and financial messaging to encourage people to eat better, quit smoking, or save for retirement.

Given the tight link between where we look and our values and priorities, it's perhaps no surprise that, as social creatures, we use other people's gaze as a cue to what's important to them. That is, we take advantage of our social partners and follow their gaze with our own eyes to identify interesting or valuable things around us. Gaze-following behavior emerges early in human development and is an important precursor of understanding the mental states of others.

Gaze-following has important consequences for managing both teams and customers. Where we look tends to shift the attention of others and subsequently nudge their choices. One study found that merely seeing an image of a person looking in the direction of a snack food increased participants' willingness to pay for the snack, without them even being aware of this effect.[131] In recent work, we asked participants to view ads in which either celebrities or attractive noncelebrities were looking toward or away from a snack-food product.[132] In subsequent preference tests, people were much more likely to choose the gazed-at product—especially if it was cued by a celebrity's gaze. These studies convincingly demonstrate that where other people look can profoundly influence how much we value a product and thus how much we are willing to pay for it. The implications for marketing are obvious.

Remarkably, we're more likely to trust people when their gaze is a more reliable predictor of important things in the environment.[133] By the same logic, mutual gaze is also a signal of trust. Looking someone in the eye says "I think you're important!" All this means that where you look matters. When you're leading a meeting or speaking with a client, be conscious of your gaze and use it to shape the conversation and, ultimately, the decision process. This goes for Zoom meetings too.

Option Fatigue and the Paradox of Choice

Think about the last time you needed to hire someone. How many applicants did you interview? How many did you screen, possibly using applicant tracking software? Recruiting and hiring consultants report that only about 2% of applicants receive job offers.[134] Hiring is one of the most important decisions a business leader has to make, yet it is also one of the most difficult—and one of the most expensive. One reason that making a good hiring decision is so challenging now is the sheer volume of applications that are submitted electronically.

Why does having more options make it more difficult to make a decision? After all, economists assert that having more options makes people happier and more satisfied because they are more likely to find the item—in this case, the job prospect—they really want. In reality, though, we experience what is often called a paradox of choice or option fatigue. This is a big problem whether you're a leader who wants to make good hiring decisions, a retailer who wants to encourage consumers to buy products, or a home buyer searching for a new house on Zillow.

The paradox of choice was first studied experimentally about 20 years ago. Sheena Iyengar of Columbia University and Mark Lepper of Stanford conducted research at Draeger's Supermarket, an upscale retailer in Menlo Park, California.[135] The store was chosen because of the incredible variety it offers its shoppers, including 250 kinds of mustard, 300 kinds of jam, and 75 types of olive oil. It also frequently sets up tasting booths, so customers are used to being able to sample some of these options.

One day, Iyengar and Lepper set up a display table with 24 different kinds of Wilkin & Sons jam. Then another day, they offered six different types of jam. They found that while the larger display generated more interest, it led to significantly fewer sales (3% vs. 30%) than the six-jam display. The conclusion? Too much choice is "demotivating."

The study has been repeated with other food items, prescription drug plans in Medicare Part D, and even mutual fund options in retirement savings plans. Iyengar found in this last study, remarkably, that when too many mutual fund options are offered, fewer people participate in the savings plan—even though it means forfeiting the money their employers would contribute (in essence, free money!).

But a few years after these results were published, new research seemed to provide more nuance to the paradox of choice. More than one study has concluded that, especially in a domain well known to the decider, more choices are preferable.[136] The debate might have gone on indefinitely if not for neuroscience research. To start, let's look at a study led by Colin Camerer at the California Institute of Technology in Pasadena.[137]

Participants were shown pictures of landscapes and asked to choose one out of a set of 6, 12, or 24 to personalize a mug or other item. While they were deciding, their brains were scanned with fMRI, which showed heightened activity in the anterior cingulate cortex, the part linked to decision-making, and in the striatum, which is linked to assessing value.

The researchers found that these brain areas were the most active in participants who chose from sets of 12 images, and that they were the least active in participants who chose from either 6 or 24 pictures. You might think that the largest number of options would be preferred, since it offers the greatest potential reward, but it's more difficult to evaluate those options (as we'll see in detail below), which might take away from the value of that reward. In other words, choosing from 12 options is good, but choosing from 24 is so difficult that we often fail to get what we really want.

Camerer concluded that an "ideal" number of options is between 8 and 15, taking into account the perceived value of the reward (will you get a significantly better picture on your mug if you can choose from 24 rather than 12 images?), the effort required to assess the options (it takes longer to choose from the larger number), and individual personality.

Our Brains Have Limits

Clearly, our brains often have trouble making decisions when confronted with lots of options. Neuroscientists have discovered that the reason for this difficulty is that there are physical limitations on the number of options we can usefully consider. Neurons can send only about 100 spikes (or "action potentials") per second, due to the energetic demands of "resetting the battery" that allows a neuron to send another spike in the first place. This physiological constraint

Figure 5.1: Titchener Circles

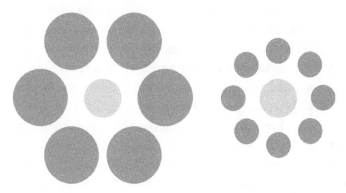

has caused our brains to become very efficient when it comes to using neuronal activity to signal information.

Our brains use a process called *divisive normalization*—science-ese for a specific kind of shortcut—to encode information. This process was first discovered in the visual system. Many optical illusions, such as in Figure 5.1 (known as the Ebbinghaus illusion or Titchener circles illusion), take advantage of normalization.[138]

Our brains tell us that the middle circle on the left is smaller, even though it's the same size as the one on the right. Our brains simply compute the size of the middle circle relative to the average sizes of the entire array of circles, making the one on the right seem larger.

We now know that divisive normalization also affects the parts of our brain that mediate our decisions. Rather than signal the absolute value or utility of the options confronting us, our brains compute the relative difference of each option from the average of all the options. And this normalization process occurs both in the moment, considering all the options in front of us, and across time, dividing out the value of options we have encountered in the recent past. In a sense, this is why 45 degrees feels cold in June and warm in December, and why a five-dollar coupon for Domino's pizza is more enticing than the same coupon would be for a Tesla.

Many studies have shown how increasing the number of options reduces the neuronal activity signaling the value of each option.

Since decision-making is an accumulation process, this means it takes longer to reach the threshold to make a choice, if we reach it at all. Ultimately, the longer it takes to make a decision, the less confident we feel about it—and the more likely we are to want to revise our choice. It turns out that the tyranny of choice is not a mere artifact of irrational psychology but instead arises from physical constraints on the processes neurons use to signal information.

Remarkably, we're now learning that this normalization process operates a little bit differently in each person. Some people, for example, are much more prone to visual illusions, like the Titchener circles shown in Figure 5.1, and it seems this may be related to the processes in the brain that implement normalization. Some recent studies show that individual differences in normalization may account for differences in how much people are influenced by framing decisions in terms of losses or gains. In the future, knowing someone's normalization function may be very useful for understanding how they will make decisions as a customer or even as an employee.

Shaping Decisions

"What's the problem?"

There's a famous scene in the movie *Moneyball*, starring Brad Pitt, in which he plays the general manager of the Oakland Athletics, a team that was leading a revolution for smaller-market teams in Major League Baseball.

In 2001, the A's had lost in heartbreaking fashion in the playoffs. And they were on the cusp of losing via free agency three of their most important players: first baseman Jason Giambi, centerfielder Johnny Damon, and relief pitcher Jason Isringhausen.

Pitt keeps asking his colleagues in the front office what their problem is. They say it's replacing these players. But as Pitt explains, the problem is bigger.

"The problem we're trying to solve is that there are rich teams and there are poor teams, then there are 50 feet of crap, and then there's us," he says. "It's an unfair game."

A key takeaway about divisive normalization (and optical illusions) is that context matters. We've already touched on this in terms of attention: Getting people to look over here means they're not looking over there, and they're more likely to choose what's here. Many marketing ploys, and even political campaigns, shape decisions by altering contexts. You may have heard of it in behavioral economics terms as the nudge theory. Either way, the idea is that by making subtle changes to the environment, you can steer people to make a decision, without them knowing they have been swayed by an outside influence. Several techniques exist for becoming that outside influence.

Pitt's soliloquy is an example of the *framing effect*—how options in a choice set are described. In other words, the options themselves are not the concern but rather how they're talked about.

Neuroscience shows that framing changes the way our brains respond to options and trigger a decision. In a now-classic study, Benedetto De Martino and Ray Dolan asked people to choose between a sure bet and a gamble, which could be framed in terms of losses or gains with respect to the amount of money at stake.[139] Just as in many prior studies, participants tended to gamble to avoid options framed as losses but were more inclined to take sure bets framed as gains. When people gambled to avoid a sure loss, their amygdalas were strongly activated. The amygdala mobilizes emotions like fear and excitement to help guide our decisions and behavior, suggesting emotions play a key role in framing. Importantly, people who naturally activated the orbitofrontal cortex, a part of the frontal lobe that integrates cognitive and emotional information supporting a decision, were less affected by framing. These findings help explain why strategies designed to regulate our emotions—for example, by "thinking like a trader"—curb our sensitivity to framing.

Then there's the *decoy effect* (also known as asymmetric dominance), in which an undesirable decoy option is added to a set of choices to drive interest in a desired option. Marketers, retailers, financial advisors, realtors, and others successfully use this effect to influence your decisions.

Three Ways to Resist Decoys

We've already discussed the trade-off between speed and accuracy, and that trade-off applies here too. To avoid being swayed by a decoy, slow down and ask yourself two questions before you make a decision:

- *What's the "unit cost" of each option?* In the grocery store, that could mean what each ounce of milk costs in a quart or gallon container. For a vacation, what's the cost per similar room in each deal? For a big-screen TV, what's the cost per inch?
- *What matters to you?* If you can't drink more than a quart before the milk goes bad, the gallon isn't a good deal. If you don't care about having a deluxe room versus a standard one, it doesn't matter that the deluxe one seems to be a better deal.

A study led by Terrence Connolly of the University of Arizona identified another highly effective way to mitigate the decoy effect: Think about how you might regret the choice you're about to make.[142] Connolly and his colleagues asked students to choose between sets of potential jobs that included a decoy. Those who first read a statement about the possibility that they might choose one that they would later regret were much less likely to choose the decoy. Just contemplating the regret you might feel by making the wrong choice can help you make a better one.

Imagine you're a wine merchant selling two wines: one for $10 and the other for $30. Most people find the $30 wine too expensive and don't buy it. Adding a much higher priced wine, say at $50, which you don't expect anyone to buy, makes the $30 wine more appealing. The normalization process causes us to see the $30 wine as above average in price in the first choice set, and therefore too expensive, but precisely at the average price in the second choice set.

A few years ago, Williams-Sonoma used this approach to nudge its customers.[140] The upscale kitchenware retailer was offering a bread maker for $279, but it wasn't selling well. Then it introduced another model that sold for $429. Sales of the original, now "less expensive" model doubled. Since most consumers don't know the wholesale value of what they're buying, they rely on normalization, taking in cues from the environment to help shape their decisions. In this case, the environment signaled that the $279 bread maker was a relative bargain.

Research shows how the decoy effect is effective in swaying decisions in politics, finance, and other sectors. One study offered a group of investors two stocks.[141] Stock A had long-term growth of 20% and a dividend yield of 2%, and stock B had long-term growth of 10% and a dividend yield of 7%. With just these two options, participants chose according to personal preference for short- or long-term gains.

A second group was offered the original two options, plus a carefully considered decoy: Stock C had long-term growth of 15% and a dividend yield of 1%. Why was this a clever decoy to sway investors to choose stock A? It was slightly worse in terms of both long-term growth and dividend yield, which made stock A look like a great choice, no matter how the participants felt about long- versus short-term gains.

The Leader's Brainwaves: Things to Remember

- Our brains weigh evidence and value to make a decision. This takes time, which is one reason it's often hard to make a good decision. If you can, slow down to make better decisions.
- When you don't have the luxury of slowing down, you have no choice but to make a trade-off between speed and accuracy. It's best in these situations to expect and tolerate some mistakes.
- Where we look and pay attention affects the decision process. This means you can nudge people's choices by making your offer or product stand out.
- As social creatures, we follow the gaze of others. Use your own gaze to guide where others look, which will subtly shape what they see and therefore choose.

- Our brains are physically limited when it comes to the number of options we can usefully consider. Be careful not to overload your employees or your customers with too many options.
- Brains save energy by calculating how different each option is from the average. You can use decoys to shape this process and nudge people's decisions.

Chapter 6

Driving Performance
Small Surprises Make It Stick

In 1989, Jack Welch, the legendary CEO of General Electric, launched a corporate revolution by hiring the world's first chief learning officer, or CLO, in Steve Kerr. Because he was a professor at USC, Kerr started out devoting just 25 days a year consulting for GE, but soon found his services in demand over 210 days per year, eventually leading him to join the company full time. Companies need to develop and implement training programs in order to adapt to the changing landscape of business, including technological innovation, and navigate organizational change.

So what does a CLO do? "I had to figure it out," Kerr is quoted as saying. "My job became to identify the barriers. What is it about the way we organize work and build rewards? What is it that keeps people from wanting to communicate, and what adjustments in rewards, and norms, and so on would create more motivation?"[143] And that job description still fits. CLOs help build a culture of learning that allows employees to advance, stay engaged, communicate effectively, and ultimately achieve the goals of the firm.

So how *do* people learn? Let's start by thinking about "learning styles." I'm giving away the punchline by putting the term in quotes. While there are plenty of tests to help you determine whether you're a visual learner (or physical, verbal, social, or one of the other purported styles), these have all largely been debunked. A study published in *Psychological Science in the Public Interest* concluded, "The contrast between the enormous popularity of the learning-styles approach within education and the lack of credible evidence for its utility is, in our opinion, striking and disturbing."[144]

What do we really know about how we learn, and how can we as leaders use that knowledge to motivate behavior and enhance performance? A number of learning processes are deeply baked into our brains, and even uber-cerebral physicists and financial analysts are at their mercy. But neuroscience is providing us with greater insights into what they are and how they work, helping us to identify when the process, and not our true intellect, is in charge. That makes it easier for us to capitalize on our baked-in learning processes and, when necessary, override them. Doing so will not only unleash peak performance but increase happiness as well.

Reinforcement Learning Runs the Show

Our brains are statistical pattern-learning devices that continuously generate updated estimates of the current state of the world. Remarkably, they do so using the same algorithm—called reinforcement learning—that is at the heart of machine learning tools that are revolutionizing business and commerce through big data.

Reinforcement learning works by comparing what we predicted with what actually happened and tries to minimize the gap between the two, known as the "reward prediction error." When reward prediction errors are large, it means the world is much better than we forecast. When they are small, the world is just about the same as we expected. And when they are zero, the world is fully predicted and there is nothing to learn. This algorithm is so efficient that it guides the behavior of every animal on the planet and has also been harnessed to support personalized advertising online, self-driving cars, and autonomous drones.

We've known since the early 1900s that reinforcement learning isn't about having an aha moment. Each experience gives us a little more information that we can use to adapt our behavior. But for all the good outcomes that are possible with reinforcement learning (if your investments in your 401(k) performed well last year you're

The Power of Lifelong Learning

As the world's population ages and lifespans increase, age-related cognitive decline and dementia have become a public health issue. Some exercises do seem to boost cognition. Researchers at Johns Hopkins studied the effects of two common brain-training methods,[146] finding that a memory sequencing game (similar to the electronic toy Simon) improved working memory by 30%. This skill is critical for performance at work, especially when dealing with new tasks that require more than old knowledge and habits. Neuroscientist and coauthor Susan Courtney says "the findings suggest that this particular task is changing something about the brain."

Nevertheless, beware of brain-training apps that promise the skills you develop will translate to other areas of your life. Penn neuroscientist Joe Kable performed a rigorous, randomized control trial of using the commercial brain-training app Lumosity on brain activity and decision-making. His group found no significant improvement in brain function or self-control, compared with playing online video games.[147] Brain training yields very specific improvements in task performance rather than any general enhancement of cognitive function.

more likely to save this year),[145] there are bad ones as well. We can thank reinforcement learning for our tendency to hold on to winning stocks too long and get rid of losing stocks too quickly—a phenomenon in economics known as the "disposition effect."

Consistency Is Key

Google's Project Oxygen gathered data about what makes a great manager and created an actionable list of 10 behaviors. Laszlo Bock, former senior vice president for people operations, said they also studied great leaders—and what they determined to be most important may surprise you. "For leaders," he explained, "it's important that people know you are consistent and fair in how you think about making decisions and that there's an element of predictability. If a leader is consistent, people on their teams experience tremendous freedom, because then they know that within certain parameters, they can do whatever they want. If your manager is all over the place, you're never going to know what you can do, and you're going to experience it as very restrictive."[148]

Dopamine Drives the Reinforcement Learning Engine

We've debunked the right brain/left brain and learning-styles theories, so now let's turn to dopamine. It's the "feel good" chemical, right?

Wrong.

Dopamine is actually involved in motivation, not rewards, and it's critically important in reinforcement learning. It fires up when there's a positive mismatch between what you expected (nothing) and what happened (unexpected food!). It basically tells you that, based on recent experience, the world is about to get much better. And any stimulus that predicts the surprisingly good outcome generates that positive mismatch—forecasting that the world is about to get a whole lot better and that we should repeat whatever behavior caused this surprisingly good outcome.

Dopamine is a very potent brain chemical. Its power is vividly illustrated by addiction and compulsive behaviors. Every drug of abuse changes dopamine signaling in some way.[149] Drugs like cocaine and amphetamines increase dopamine levels, thus magnifying positive reward prediction errors and making the world seem a whole lot better than expected. This is how drug-taking—and other behaviors like gambling that amplify dopamine—hijacks our brains, leading to addiction.[150]

The powerful role of dopamine in learning is also made plain by disorders that affect dopamine. Parkinson's disease results in progressive degeneration and death of the 200,000 dopamine neurons in the brain. This results not only in the halting movements and tremors that characterize the disease but also in impairments in learning and decision-making.[151]

Parkinson's disease is typically treated by giving drugs that replenish dopamine. Unfortunately, it's difficult to fine-tune this process for each individual. In the late 1990s, case reports began to surface in the medical literature of Parkinson's patients who showed bizarre changes in behavior after being treated with dopamine-boosting drugs.[152] For example, one conservative minister treated with dopamine drugs gambled away his church's assets on lottery tickets. Dopamine therapy can also trigger compulsive eating, shopping, and even demands for sex from the patient's partner or others.[153]

These stunning observations make it very clear that the dopamine-driven reinforcement learning engine in our brains is so powerful it can change our very personalities. As we'll see, this learning engine shapes nearly every aspect of our behavior, often in subtle but detectable ways that we're not even aware of.

The Optimism Bias

Have you ever noticed that when you're in a good mood you're more likely to make what I've labeled in this chapter a positive prediction error? You expect a good outcome, even when you know the chance for that outcome may be slim. Also known as the optimism bias, it's the reason why you are more prone to risk-taking when things are going well.

An interesting study at New York University looked at data on local sports teams, noting days on which a team was expected to lose but won.[154] On those days, people across the city purchased more lottery tickets. The researchers also looked at data on weather. On days that were sunnier than those in the recent past, lottery ticket purchases also rose. This study, and others like it, found that positive mood reflects positive prediction errors—and more gambling. In fact, lottery ticket purchases were a linear function of reward prediction errors calculated from recent sports team performance as well as recent weather.

Building on these studies, new work shows that people's moment-to-moment happiness tracks positive prediction errors in their daily lives.[155] One important implication of this is that we can be happier by systematically *lowering* our expectations. Doing so makes it easier to create positive prediction errors, leading to the brief bursts of dopamine that make the world look just a little bit brighter than it did before.

Recall from chapter 5 how the amount of attention we pay to an option changes how much we value it. Attention can also dial up the positive prediction errors we compute from an experience and dial down the negative ones.[156] Cassie Mogilner Holmes of UCLA's Anderson School of Management has found that people are happier when they are primed to treat the weekend like a vacation.[157] This gets people to focus more on fun experiences and less on chores for a couple of days. This generates positive prediction errors that make the world seem a little rosier when people return to work on Monday. Unfortunately, given what we know about reinforcement learning, we would also expect people to revert back to a less happy mindset after a couple of days back on the job.

What does all this mean for leaders? For one thing, your employees and your customers won't always respond rationally to the information you give them. The uber-powerful reinforcement learning engine in their brains is always on, subtly shaping habits, motivating risk-taking or risk-aversion, and swaying happiness.

You can harness this engine by frequently giving praise to your employees for small accomplishments at work. Wharton professor Adam Grant and Francesca Gino found that employees who received gratitude from their managers subsequently worked harder and were more productive.[158] A Gallup poll conducted in 2006 found that employees who had been praised for work in the past week showed 10%–20% greater productivity. Conversely, those who had not received praise said they were three times as likely to quit in the next year as they were to stay.[159] Praise is often most effective when it is surprising—a positive reward prediction error—and when it's sincere and authentic. Best of all, recognition for a job well done doesn't cost a thing.[160]

Regrets: We've All Learned from a Few

In the hit 1950s' television series *Dragnet*, Detective Joe Friday methodically solved crimes by slowly accumulating knowledge of what really happened, famously stating, "All we want are the facts, ma'am."[161] That's analogous to reinforcement learning. But that's not the only way we learn. Neuroscience has revealed some of the mechanisms that allow us to reflect on our experiences as well as the choices we didn't make to imagine what might have been.

Fictive, or counterfactual, learning takes place in our imagination, when we realize what would have happened if we had made a different choice. This type of learning is often linked to feelings of regret (the "coulda, woulda, shoulda" line of thinking), but it can also happen when we realize a choice we didn't make would have been much better.

Fictive learning helps us take into account more information from the environment than learning from direct experience alone. But it can only improve our decision-making if there are statistical dependencies between what one observes and what might happen in the future. This is powerfully demonstrated by the fact that gamblers often shift their bets when they observe that they could have won more money on a different option—as when roulette players move their bets from black to red after seeing the ball land there. Of course, this strategy is ineffective because each roll of the roulette wheel is independent (assuming it's a fair table).

It's difficult to ignore fictive information, because this system is so deeply baked into our brains. Other animals, including monkeys and rats, also learn from foregone outcomes. We once ran an experiment in which monkeys played a version of roulette by making bets on which of eight slots would yield a jackpot.[162] Just like people, monkeys shifted their bets whenever they saw that they could have done better by choosing a different option. And the bigger the fictive "error," the more likely monkeys were to shift their bets—just like people.

People, monkeys, and rats learn from fictive information by using the same brain mechanisms. Professors Terry Lohrenz, Read

Montague, and Colin Camerer developed a stock market task in which people could decide on each round how much money to put into stocks or cash. Then, they received feedback telling them whether the market went up or down. When people observed that they could have done better by putting more money into the market on the previous round, they shifted more money into stocks—just like roulette players. Other studies using similar tasks show that fictive learning has a strong and pervasive effect on human decision-making.[163]

Evidence shows that a network of areas in the brain's cerebral cortex supports fictive learning and the regret we often feel when we learn we could have made a better decision.[164] Two of these areas—the upper part of the anterior cingulate cortex along the midline of the frontal lobe, and the insula buried beneath the folds of the frontal and temporal cortex—are triggered when we observe that we could have done better by making a different choice. We also found that single neurons in the anterior cingulate signaled precisely how much better monkeys could have done by choosing differently,[165] and this signal predicted the likelihood they would change their bets on the next round.

These signals percolate down to the reinforcement learning engine, which as we've already seen is itself informed about reward prediction errors generated by dopamine neurons based on direct experience. Remarkably, fictive learning signals can be affected in addiction and altered by our beliefs. Smokers' brains generate fictive error signals in the reinforcement learning circuit just as non-smokers' brains do. But smokers don't respond to these signals, and tend to ignore what might have been if they had made a different decision.

This decoupling may account for why it's so difficult to quit smoking—for some reason it's difficult to use "coulda, woulda, shoulda" information to make a better choice. It also suggests that smokers may make better investors, a finding corroborated in a recent study.[166] Using the same stock market game, the researchers found that despite the fact that smokers' brains generate fictive error signals when they see the market go up after putting money into cash, they don't change their investments on the next trial.

Just like reinforcement learning, the fictive learning circuit in our brains is always on. That means that the behavior and decisions of our leaders, our employees, our teammates, and our customers reflect not only what they learn from direct experience but also what they didn't choose and what they imagine might have happened if they did.

Again, this isn't necessarily a bad thing. Remember that the ability to learn from unchosen or imagined alternatives evolved for a good reason, namely because it allows us to go beyond direct experience and make better decisions in the future. Knowing when to rely on such counterfactual thinking—and detaching ourselves from the emotional baggage of regret—is the key to getting it right. In fact, Wharton professor Phil Tetlock and Haas Business School professor Laura Kray found that people who were able to imagine more possible outcomes in the past were better at forecasting the probabilities of future events[167]—an important trait for any leader.

Think Like a Trader

A study asked people to perform the sequential investment game we've already learned about.[168] The authors first showed that some people are more strongly influenced by fictive errors, while others rely much more on direct reinforcement learning. Amazingly, priming the fictive learners to "regulate" by focusing on the entire sequence of choices and overall performance, rather than attending to each and every outcome, reduced the impact of fictive information on their decisions.

In essence, the best strategy is to "think like a trader." Specifically, remember that "you take risks with money every day, for a living. All that matters is that you come out on top in the end—a loss or gain here or there will not matter in terms of your overall portfolio. In other words, you win some and you lose some."

A prior study showed this advice to be effective in reducing loss aversion as well.[169] Thinking like a trader decoupled signaling between the insula and the striatum, where fictive errors and reward prediction errors are combined to drive learning and decision-making. This is another example of how stepping back, slowing down, and seeing the whole picture can help us make better decisions.

Learning by Observing Others

Humans and some other social animals learn from watching others and thinking about their experiences. Other people (and other animals) provide a rich source of fictive information about the world that we can use to learn and improve our decision-making. Seeing how someone else's choice worked for them gives us information we can tap into later when we have to make our own choice.

This kind of social learning is crucial for human culture and technology, allowing for the transmission of information from person to person and generation to generation. It's the key to the human adaptive tool kit. Unfortunately, it can also affect our decisions, sometimes with massive economic consequences.

Perhaps the most obvious case is the phenomenon of herding in financial markets. Herding occurs when we copy the decisions other people make. If we see our neighbor profit in the stock market, we're more likely to invest some of our own money. This causes the market to go up, which triggers herding by other investors. Over time, this leads to a bubble in which investors drive the price of the stock above its fundamental value. Of course, bubbles are unstable and eventually burst, leaving investors with steep losses.

As we learned in chapter 3, the social brain network manages our connections with others. One part of this network, in the inferior part of the anterior cingulate cortex, signals the rewards and punishments experienced by others. In addition to generating the feeling of empathy, these signals also allow us to learn from the experiences of others. A second part of this network, including the temporo-parietal junction and dorsomedial prefrontal cortex, mediates our ability to think about what others want, believe, and know and allows us to make predictions about their behavior. Scientists have found that activation of this "mentalizing" circuit when performing the sequential stock market task leads to herding and the formation of bubbles.

Again, it's astonishing how deeply baked in these mechanisms seem to be. We taught monkeys to play a symbolic version of the sequential stock market game.[170] Monkeys saw the price of a stock, could see their holdings, and then decided whether to buy more stock, stick with what they had, or cash in—for juice, not money, of course. Just like humans, monkeys tended to buy more stocks when their price was going up. And both monkeys and humans were more likely to buy stocks when they were trading in the market with another investor. We found that neurons in the monkey "mentalizing network" forecast the decision to buy, and these signals were amplified in social markets.

If even monkeys can't help but get sucked into financial bubbles by their social brain networks, how in the world can we avoid it? For leaders, there are two answers. First, it will take effort and training. Slow down, weigh the options, and settle in for the long term. In other words, think like a trader (see the above sidebar). Second, different jobs benefit from different talents, traits, and motivators. Understanding which jobs require social sensitivity and which jobs are impaired by it, and how to measure this capability, is critical for assembling the right workforce.

Neurodiversity and Leadership Decisions

One of the most important decisions a business leader makes is hiring the right person for the right job and giving them the support and development to reach their full potential. Doing so requires knowing what each job really entails and understanding each person's talents, traits, and motivators. As we've seen throughout this book, one of the most important things neuroscience has discovered in the past decade is that people really do differ in the way their brains make decisions, in how they get along with others, and in how they think creatively. These differences are the product of nature and nurture—the way that an individual's genetic endowment interacts with the environment to shape brain structure and function. Tapping into these talents presents an enormous opportunity for business leaders willing to embrace neuroscience and other analytics to understand human potential.

One good example is financial decision-making. We now know that people who are on the autism spectrum appear to have less divisive normalization in their brains than those without autism (see chapter 5 for a refresher). This makes them less susceptible to certain visual illusions, and less affected by framing effects in financial decisions. Similarly, we found that people who scored low on social sensitivity tests developed to quantify social impairments in autism made the best financial decisions in our sequential stock market—precisely because they engaged less in thinking about other investors' successes and what they were going to do next.

Overall, these findings suggest that people on the autism spectrum may make ideal stock traders and financial analysts. The Centers for Disease Control and Prevention estimates that roughly 1 in 59 children born in the United States is on the autism spectrum. This translates into 70,000 teenagers with autism transitioning into adulthood each year—and fewer than half of them will hold jobs by age 25.[171] This is a pool of untapped human potential that could help companies alleviate talent shortages in the coming decade. The opportunities presented by other neurodiverse populations, including ADHD, obsessive-compulsive disorder (OCD), and bipolar, are clear for companies willing to learn about the unique talents and drives of these populations.

The Leader's Brainwaves: Things to Remember

- Our brains are wired to learn from trial and error, regret, and observing the choices other people make. These processes operate continuously and affect many of the decisions we make every day, without us being aware of it.

- Whether it's Pavlov's dog getting a food reward every time the bell rings or a manager who always rewards innovative thinking, consistency helps us learn and make adjustments much more quickly.
- We're happier and more optimistic when things turn out just a little better than expected. We can rev up these positive prediction errors by focusing our attention on good outcomes and experiences and ignoring the bad ones.
- Think like a trader to minimize the impact of regret and counterfactual thinking on your decisions. Slow down, take a deep breath, and adopt a long-term mindset.
- Being a good leader requires good social skills. But beware the herd mentality that accompanies paying too much attention to what other people choose.
- Consider the untapped talent pool of cognitively diverse populations who may be wired to perform better than others in certain jobs. Less social people, for example, may make better investors.

Chapter 7

The Future of Brain Science in Business
How to Turn It Up to 11

It's Game 7 of the World Series between the New York Yankees and the Los Angeles Dodgers. The Yankees' starting pitcher trots out to the mound to pitch the bottom of the ninth. He looks good, and he says he feels great. But data from a miniature EEG in his hat, as well as smart sensors in his shirt that track his heart rate and the content of his sweat, trigger an algorithm that sends an alert to his manager. Despite a low pitch count, his ace has become distracted due to mental fatigue. The manager asks the pitcher for the ball and calls the bullpen to bring in a relief pitcher. The EEG saved the game and, in this case, the season, propelling the Yankees to a championship.

This scenario may seem far-fetched, but I assure you it's not. As neuroscientists continue to develop new technologies, make new discoveries, and consider new applications of their findings, we are on the cusp of revolutionary advances in using these tools to enhance performance at work and improve well-being at home. In this chapter, we'll look at some of the exciting developments and potential outcomes stemming from neuroscience breakthroughs, especially as the field merges new technologies with algorithms and big data. We'll also consider the ethical, legal, and societal implications of these developments and explore evolving best practices.

Performance enhancement—for individuals, teams, or companies—surfaces a host of important questions that we, as a society, must grapple with to ensure we apply new insights and technologies in a fair, just, and transparent way.

Fitbits for Your Brain

Brain science has advanced in lockstep with the development of new technologies for monitoring and manipulating brain activity, as well as the development of new computational tools for analyzing the data. Nevertheless, much of the near future of neuroscience applications for business and human potential will leverage wearable versions of existing technologies.

For example, we've discussed EEGs. They've been used in labs and clinics since 1924. But while they are an effective way to noninvasively monitor the brain, their size, wetness (standard EEGs require electroconductive gels), setup time, and cost have restricted their potential uses. Over the past decade, though, technology and design breakthroughs have led to direct-to-consumer, wearable EEGs that can record brain signals while people are engaged in regular activities.

I have focused a lot on sports in this book, and in our work in general, because I believe sports is a great petri dish for business, and for life in general. Sports outcomes are easier to measure objectively, and small improvements in performance can have a huge impact in terms of winning or losing, investing in the wrong player, or putting together a lineup with poor team chemistry.

Big data revolutionized coaching decisions in baseball, followed by many other sports. "Moneyball"-type approaches inform coaching decisions about recruiting, training, and the lineup based on models applied to the statistics of prior performance. In the future, coaching decisions could be enhanced by neuroscience data (as well as other biological information) providing objective measures of cognitive and emotional tendencies (you might call this "Neuro-Moneyball"). Advances in miniaturization, mobility, and affordability mean a coach could know when a particular player might peak or which potential recruits are most likely to thrive under pressure.

In addition to the study of University of Pennsylvania rowers discussed in chapter 2, my team and I used our own wearable EEGs while working with a professional UK soccer team to evaluate players' focus during training drills, susceptibility to stress under pressure, and ability to predict and outwit opponents. Preliminary analyses suggest some of these data predict on-field performance. As of this writing, we are conducting a study with the Penn wrestling team to measure the impact of extreme physical fatigue on the neural signals underlying decision-making and competitiveness.

In business, the same kinds of data could be used to determine job placement and hiring decisions, training and development, employee onboarding, and team management. There are huge ethical implications with this, and we'll get to that later in this chapter.

But the impact of neuroscience and related big data analytics is not limited to management decisions. It extends to other applications as well, such as customer experience, brand strategy, and even finance. For example, we conducted a study with a major European business-to-business software corporation. For a focus group attending a trade show, we found that EEG data helped predict which booths and activities people would visit and which keynotes would be most engaging. The current gold standard is emailing attendees a survey after the conference, which is a poor measure of customer experience. But now we have exciting results showing, for example, that social interactions move the needle more than any other trade show experience, and that some speakers really aren't worth investing in for keynote speeches.

Wearable sensor technology also has the clear potential to revolutionize mental health. Medical wearables could be used for in-home seizure monitoring for children and for mental health, to watch for changes in state of mind that might indicate anxiety or depression, or to provide objective readouts on pharmacological treatment of psychiatric disorders. In our lab, for example, we were able to identify subclinical anxiety with about 84% accuracy using algorithms that combined EEG data with pupil responses, heart rate variability, and skin conductance. We also found that brain data provided deeper insights into the way participants responded to stress, in ways that were often missed by self-reported feelings.

NeuroFlow—a connected health start-up spun out of Wharton and Penn by CEO Chris Molaro and COO Adam Pardes—incorporates EEG and other biological data into continuous medical records of medical and psychological therapy to help doctors make better decisions for their patients and to give patients a deeper sense of ongoing changes in their brain states during treatment.

In addition to wearable sensors, we are seeing advances in implantable technologies, which have been around since the 1970s. Brain-machine interfaces (BMIs) and brain computer interfaces (BCIs) have made it possible for monkeys to control robotic arms, and paralyzed people to move cursors on a screen. In 2012, implants into paralyzed patients' motor cortexes allowed them to direct the motion of a robotic arm, performing fine-motor skills, like drinking a cup of coffee, with great precision. There is no doubt that BMIs and BCIs can be life-changing for people with movement disorders that limit their mobility and autonomy.

Wharton alum and mega-entrepreneur Elon Musk wants to take the technology even further. He founded Neuralink in 2016 and three years later unveiled a microchip that can record brain activity and, potentially, stimulate it.[172] Ultimately, the goal is to link the chip to artificial intelligence and potentially connect your brain directly to the internet, allowing you to upload and download information at will, seamlessly, without a manual user interface.

Neuroscientists express significant skepticism about the plausibility of this idea. But it is based on solid science showing that our brains, and those of animals, can incorporate new signals and use the information to guide behavior. BMI pioneer Miguel Nicolelis, a former colleague of mine at Duke University, showed that implanting an infrared sensor on the head of a mouse, plugging it into its brain, and then training the animal to associate activation of the sensor with food essentially endowed the animal with the ability to "see" heat. Normally, mice can't do that. It's a big leap from a simple heat sensor to the vastness of the internet, but it's perhaps not as far-fetched an idea as it seems.

Turning the Brain Up to 11

Can you buy a better brain? There are drugs and other so-called neuroenhancers on the market that claim to give you greater clarity, memory, focus, and control—and people are buying them. Imagine getting more and better work done in half the time, making superior decisions, and keeping your cool during intense meetings and phone calls because you took a pill or spent time earlier in the day with an electrical stimulator strapped to your head. To paraphrase the character Nigel Tufnel in the 1984 mockumentary *This Is Spinal Tap*, can we turn our brains up to 11?

Nigel was referring to his Marshall guitar amplifiers, which went up to 11 instead of 10, leading Nigel to *believe* they were louder than standard amplifiers, though they actually just gave the same output. This is an important concept to keep in mind when evaluating brain enhancements that purport to improve function. If a neuroenhancer merely serves to make you *think* you have increased performance, then at best you've bought into a placebo. While placebo effects can be powerful, I don't think most people would want to invest time and money in an enhancement that doesn't actually work.

With that caveat in mind, it's clear that neuroscience is making exciting advances in techniques for stimulating and manipulating brain function. Most of these advancements are currently directed at helping people restore functions that are lost or impaired, rather than enhancing functions in otherwise healthy people. For example, transcranial magnetic stimulation (TMS) is a technique that uses strong magnetic fields to induce electrical currents in the brain. The currents can either turn on or turn off specific brain areas, and these modulations then ripple to downstream brain regions, and the brain can make lasting changes in response to these treatments. Research is currently being done with TMS on depression, migraine, pain management, and other neurological disorders. TMS works, but not always; however, it's expensive and currently limited to medical applications.

Transcranial direct-current stimulation (tDCS), by contrast, delivers a tiny electric current directly to the scalp, which also seems to change brain activity. This is essentially the same thing as wiring a battery across your head, and many folks in the DIY community are experimenting with just that. There is some controversy regarding how tDCS works—whether it directly affects brain activity where the stimulation is applied or whether it has broader, brain-wide effects by activating or deactivating arousal systems. Clinically, tDCS is being explored to treat depression, schizophrenia, aphasia, addiction, epilepsy, chronic pain (migraine, fibromyalgia), attention deficit disorder, and motor impairments. The most popular consumer tDCS device is probably Halo, which claims to improve athletes' physical performance by strengthening connections between the brain's motor areas and the muscles, and musicians' instrument-playing skills by enhancing fine-motor skills. It may have business applications as well. For example, tDCS applied to the front of the head, over the prefrontal cortex, can alter risk preferences and change how you respond to unfair offers, with clear potential applications to finance and business.

There are many other technologies currently available or in development that may eventually offer ordinary people the ability to directly manipulate their own brain functions. Some may deliver performance enhancement, and some may not. As long as there are technologies available that might enhance performance, people will use them. The question we need to ask ourselves, as individuals and as a society, is, Should they? And if so, under what conditions? And if we do accept the use of neuroscience to enhance performance, how do we level the playing field?

Lessons from *Minority Report*

How do we decide whether it's okay to use neuroscience to improve business or enhance performance? Consider the provocative and very prescient short story *Minority Report*, written in 1956 by Philip K. Dick. In the story, it's 2054. John Anderton—played by

Tom Cruise in the 2002 movie version—joins an elite policing unit known as Pre-crime, which has been able to completely eliminate murders in Washington, DC. The unit includes three people, "pre-cogs," who can see future crimes. Their visions are shared with Pre-crime officers who then identify the murderer and make an arrest. But are the pre-cogs always right? And if they're not, how many innocent people end up in jail?

At its heart, this story questions what we value as a society. In many ways, these are the same sorts of questions we're asking when we consider the application of neuroscience to business, law, and peak performance.

On August 1, 1966, former Marine Charles Whitman barricaded himself on the observation deck of the Main Building tower at the University of Texas at Austin with a cache of rifles and other weapons. Over the next hour and a half, he shot and killed 14 people and injured 31 others before he was finally overpowered and killed. An autopsy found that Whitman had a brain tumor in the white matter near his amygdala, a critical structure for managing emotions.[173] Is it possible that the tumor caused or intensified his violent impulses? If the tumor had been discovered earlier, could the tragedy have been avoided?

In the 1960s, there wasn't any way to noninvasively determine whether an individual had a brain tumor. Today, of course, MRI and CT scans offer the ability to assess many aspects of brain function—not just to detect severe neurological problems that might predispose one to violence, but also to examine other features of brain structure and function that could impact performance. Consider ethical behavior. Recent history is rife with examples of unsavory and even immoral behavior by CEOs and other business leaders, with profound impacts on company image, social welfare, and ultimately financial performance. Should we want to avoid the next Elizabeth Holmes, founder and CEO of now-defunct Theranos, who was charged with massive fraud by the Securities and Exchange Commission after the company's "breakthrough" blood-testing technology turned out to be a well-funded hoax?

Maybe the bigger question is, Can we? Recent research suggests that the answer is yes.[174] Mark Korczykowski, John Detre, and Diana Robertson from the Penn Department of Radiology and the Department of Legal Studies at Wharton studied the brains of MBA candidates and their moral development. The students were given tests of moral reasoning ability, which focused on what you consider when making decisions that could affect you and others. They found that the connections between the ventromedial prefrontal cortex and the amygdala were stronger in MBA students with higher levels of moral reasoning, consistent with an enhanced ability to deal with conflicting moral dilemmas. We still don't know if stronger connections allowed some MBA students to develop higher levels of moral reasoning or, conversely, whether exercising higher-level moral reasoning strengthened the connections. This is a critical question for determining whether education and training in moral reasoning could be used to help develop better leaders.

These findings suggest a simple brain scan may identify individuals who may be less willing or able to make sound moral decisions. They raise an interesting question of whether we should routinely include brain scans to evaluate fitness for senior leadership. They also, of course, raise even more questions around the privacy of the individuals whose brains would be scanned.

MRI and CT scans are costly—about $500 to $1,000 per hour. But for major businesses, millions or billions of dollars and the health or livelihood of thousands of employees or patients are routinely at stake.

Where We Are Now

Today, we can take people into the lab, wire them up to EEGs and eye trackers, show them ads or play music, see how they respond, and predict ticket sales and downloads—out of a sample and across the entire market. These insights have the potential to upend the ways we target consumers and, more broadly, conduct business. Are we crossing a line?

There's growing concern about the use of neuroscience in marketing. As researchers develop a greater understanding of how purchasing decisions are made, and we make advances toward manipulating consumer behavior, the fear is that marketers will be able to push your "buy button" so hard that you will purchase things you don't want or need.

Savvy marketers are using neuroscience data to make ads and packaging more appealing, for example. As we've discussed, they can activate the social brain network by including smiling faces to sell more of everything, from toothpaste to TVs. They also measure biomarkers while people are shown multiple logo and package designs, and print and digital ads in order to choose the most effective ones.

Neuromarketers get these data from people who provide their consent, but as their techniques become less obtrusive, that could change. One of the biggest scandals of the past decade breaching privacy and consent involved Cambridge Analytica, the now-defunct British political consulting firm, which obtained personal data from up to 87 million Facebook users by luring just 270,000 to use an app called This is Your Digital Life. The latter group consented to sharing information, but their friends (about 87 million) did not. Cambridge Analytica used the data to develop a complex understanding of users' personalities and then sold its findings to political groups—notably Donald Trump's 2016 presidential campaign, which used it to microtarget voters.

Wharton marketing professor Gideon Nave got access to the same data as Cambridge Analytica and showed just how powerfully it could predict personality.[175] With access to just three "likes" of music on Facebook, he could accurately predict personality types along five major dimensions. (Did you really think you weren't leaving a personally revealing digital footprint with your likes?) If you liked 10 pieces of music, he could make that prediction better than your coworker could. It went up from there to 300 likes, at which he could predict better than your spouse. And from personality, Nave could predict precisely which brands people preferred and even which music they like. This is the kind of "consent" many of us are willing to give when we share our preferences online—albeit without understanding the ways in which our information can be used.

All these examples point to two questions: How far are we willing to go? Will we know when we get there? The problem in many cases is that neuroscience data—just like other kinds of data—can be used clandestinely. But even with transparency and informed consent, as Facebook proves, can't we still go too far? We already know that awareness doesn't necessarily lead to changes in behavior.

Can we determine what a good use of the data is, and what isn't?

Can You Expand Your Mind?

My view, and the view of many of my colleagues, is that using data—whether digital footprints or EEGs—to more effectively target and persuade consumers can be a good thing. Getting the right product in front of the right person at the right time not only benefits the company but also saves the consumer time and attention and potentially helps them find a product that will make them happier. Moreover, once you've persuaded someone to try something, if they don't like it, they are unlikely to buy it again. That's simple reinforcement learning, one of the oldest tricks in the brain's tool kit.

Even so, neuroscience research into effective advertising doesn't have to be used to persuade people to buy unnecessary goods or services. The same data can be applied for the public good. A recent study of ads for microloans on Kiva's website found that those featuring a smiling person, which activates the social brain network, get much more money.[176] It makes me wonder why Kiva still features ads of frowning people if the organization knows the picture is causing them to miss out on loans.

Falk, the professor at Penn's Annenberg School for Communication whose research we discussed in chapter 3, has used neuromarketing to persuade people to engage in healthier behaviors.[177] She studied brain data of people who were viewing public service announcements that encouraged them to stop smoking, exercise, or eat healthier. She found that the parts of the brain involved in self-relevance and positive motivation are affected differently by different types of ads, and was able to predict click-through rates for ads based on these findings. The ads were then optimized for maximum effectiveness.

That's one way to make the brain more receptive to information it doesn't want to hear. But Falk took her work a step further by exploring "mind-expanding" exercises that could work like the optimized public service announcements.[178] The data are quite compelling.

The first exercise involves affirmations. People were told to think about a value that is most important to them, such as family, spirituality, or community, and then to think about how that value helped them through a difficult time. The second exercise, called compassion priming, asked people to repeatedly and vividly wish something good for a specific person. Both techniques prime the brain areas responsible for self-reference and valuing information, making people more receptive to health messages. The effect wasn't just temporary. Falk was able to predict how active people who participated in the experiment (who wore activity monitors for months after the lab session) would be by looking at how effective they were at the priming activities, based on brain activation. Astonishingly, some of them remained more active for up to three months.

These kinds of priming techniques can help people become healthier by overcoming the natural tendency to tune out information they don't want to hear—but priming can also do more. Think about the kinds of information you may need to share with your team that they won't want to hear. Priming people can make them more receptive (or at least less hostile) to news of organizational changes, budget cuts, or an impending merger.

Most people would agree that persuading people to be more active, quit smoking, and eat healthier is a desirable outcome. But some people may be perfectly happy engaging in activities that are unhealthy. Of course, there are good economic arguments for reducing the financial and social costs these behaviors impose on the rest of the public. These tensions require a balance between what's good for society and individual autonomy. The same balance is required when companies have to decide how far to go in persuading employees to take a pay cut for the good of the firm—an unfortunate consequence of economic downturns caused by the financial meltdown of 2008 and the 2020 pandemic.

How Do We Know When We've Crossed a Line?

Practitioners are beginning to address finding the balance between what's good for society or the company and what's good for the individual. In the relatively new interdisciplinary field of "neurolaw," practitioners and academics are considering how neuroscience should (and should not) be used in the legal field. As of yet, though, no standards have been developed. The same is true for other fields, such as education and medicine.

But one industry has developed what it calls "neurostandards." The Advertising Research Foundation's guidelines embrace neuroscience as an effective marketing tool, while also maintaining that its use be academically rigorous, transparent, and respectful of individuals' privacy. The latter two points are becoming increasingly important as neuroscience techniques become less invasive. The neurostandards make clear that collecting data about consumers without their knowledge or consent, and potentially using those data to manipulate them, crosses an ethical boundary.

There are also general recommendations that were established at the federal level. In April 2013, then president Barack Obama launched the Brain Research through Advancing Innovative Neurotechnologies (BRAIN) Initiative to revolutionize our understanding of the human brain. The initiative included a bioethics commission, which was charged with identifying ethical issues that could arise from neuroscience research and the application and implications of its findings. Chaired by Amy Gutmann, president of the University of Pennsylvania, the commission offered 14 recommendations, including the following:

- Informed consent and transparency
- Maintenance of human dignity
- Autonomy (don't take away people's ability to make decisions)
- Privacy
- Security
- Equal access
- Avoidance of hype

The recommendations were released in 2015, and they remain relevant and important guidelines for best practices that can be used in many industries.

The Future Is Fast and Diverse

The United States experienced steep job losses early in the COVID-19 pandemic, with more than 40 million adults filing jobless claims amid shutdowns across much of the nation. Remarkably, some companies actually *increased* hiring during the same period. Walmart hired upward of 235,000 and Amazon added over 125,000 workers. Not only were these huge numbers of people to screen, interview, and onboard, but the pace of this process was unprecedented. It required Walmart and Amazon to radically change their hiring practices by employing artificial intelligence and advanced analytics, as well as using recruitment process outsourcing firms like Korn Ferry.

Although it's hard to imagine while in the middle of the pandemic-induced employment contraction, the economy will recover. That means hundreds of companies will be competing to recruit top talent at the same time.[179] And, like Walmart and Amazon, many companies will need to hire quickly. As all savvy recruiters realize, however, hiring more quickly risks hiring the wrong person for the wrong job. All those bad hires are costly in terms of both time and money—up to $15,000 on average, according to a 2017 survey by CareerBuilder.[180] Moreover, many of the hot jobs of the next decade may be radically different from the ones in demand over the past 10 years. And the pandemic has the potential to reshape, build up, or extinguish entire industries.

All these dynamics highlight the need for more advanced tools to help recruiters and hiring managers evaluate potential employees with greater speed and precision. Walmart and Amazon have already discovered the need to engage artificial intelligence and advanced analytics to better measure the talents, traits, and motivators of job applicants and match them to the right positions. Neuroscience can help inform these tool kits. We've already discussed the ways in which neuroscience and related analytics can more precisely identify a person's social skills, decision-making limits, and innovative potential. There will be a trade-off, however, between the invasiveness of some neuroscience measures and how precisely we can predict an individual's talents, traits, and motivators. The next step will most likely involve the application of non-verbal behavioral assessments, eye tracking, video analysis, and tone of voice measures that have been validated by neuroscience to aid in talent evaluation. Naturally, the principles of consent, privacy, security, autonomy, and dignity will be more important than ever in this process.

As companies begin to contemplate hiring for the new normal and near future, they would be wise to think more broadly about the talent pool. Employers continue to disregard certain populations, even though there's strong evidence that these potential hires could perform well, as we've discussed. In chapter 5, we explored the link between ADHD and creativity. That's just one of the capabilities of people with neurological differences of which we're now aware. In the future, researchers need to identify more of these talents so we can better match neurologically diverse populations with the right jobs.

In business, embracing neurodiversity (the need to respect neurological differences just as we should with variations in race, gender, and ethnicity) isn't just about doing the right thing—it's about building the workforce you need. For example, in 2018, the Centers for

Disease Control and Prevention reported that about 1 in 59 children is diagnosed with an autism spectrum disorder (ASD).[181] Over the next 10 years, half a million of them will enter adulthood. Yet, 85% of college graduates affected by an ASD are unemployed,[182] a missed opportunity for those graduates and their would-be employers.

On the training side, the military is addressing new needs with a novel program built on neuroscience advances. Recognizing that the tools and weapons of war have advanced but training has not, DARPA (Defense Advanced Research Projects Agency) is introducing the MBA (Measuring Biological Aptitude) program.[183] Its goal is to help service members access and track signaling networks (genetic, epigenetic, and metabolomics) to achieve peak performance. It also recognizes that traditional ways of selecting people for advanced careers in the military may overlook people with talents who might actually do a better job.

The Leader's Brainwaves: Things to Remember

- Neuroscience offers the potential to revolutionize human performance through new tools and applications. Like any performance enhancer, these tools demand extra scrutiny—not just in terms of whether and how they work but whether we as a society think their use is good and fair.
- The ethical, legal, and societal implications of applying neuroscience to human performance, at home and in the workplace, have only just begun to be appreciated.
- At minimum, any application of neuroscience to improve performance or shape consumer behavior must respect privacy, consent, autonomy, human dignity, and equal access. These principles raise thorny issues for capitalist economies that thrive on competition but where there may not be equal access to the technology.
- Businesses that embrace neurodiversity by respecting and hiring for neurological differences may be able to build better workforces.

Conclusion

We've covered a lot of ground in this book—from leadership, to communication, to innovation, to learning and decision-making. We've seen that despite the fact that our brains are made up of about 80 billion neurons that make more than 100 trillion connections with each other, we are surprisingly limited in our ability to process information. Physiological constraints have forced our brains, through evolution, to be highly efficient—by signaling contrast from the background and amplifying the most important or salient information at the expense of everything else. This efficiency leads to surprising impacts on decision-making, including the tyranny of choice and the connection between where we look and what we choose. What were previously considered to be anomalies or irrationalities by economists and psychologists are better understood as the completely rational product of the evolutionary process—a perspective often termed "bounded rationality."[184]

And our brains' priorities reflect the kinds of challenges our ancestors had to solve to survive and reproduce. That includes learning from experience, as well as observing what might have been, breaking out of so-so routines to find something better, and communicating what we've learned and what we've discovered to others. These solutions are deeply baked into our brains, in systems and circuits we share with other animals, particularly our closest cousins, the monkeys and apes.

Perhaps nowhere is this clearer than when we consider the ways our brains are specialized for connecting with others. We depend on our friends and family for support through thick and thin. And, consequently, the better and deeper our connections, the healthier, happier, and, remarkably, wealthier we are. We have learned many important lessons from our monkey cousins, but this may be the most profound. Our brains' social networks manage not only our connections with our friends and family but also how we work with teammates in the office, inspire loyalty to our companies and brands, and lead through the sometimes gut-wrenching changes increasingly forced on organizations by globalization, by the rapid pace of technological change, and now, in particular, by the global pandemic of 2020.

Organizational change really is stressful. A 2017 study by the American Psychological Association found that more than 50% of surveyed employees said they had experienced extreme stress due to major changes at work.[185] Many of these folks brought this stress home, where it impacted their family life, increased sick days, and fueled drinking, smoking, and other bad behaviors.

In this light, it's inspiring and instructive to think back to the rhesus macaques on Cayo Santiago Island that endured the intense impact of Hurricane Maria and the lingering physical and social hardships in its aftermath. At the time of this writing, we have been observing the monkeys for almost three years after the hurricane. As I discussed in the introduction, the monkeys have responded by becoming even more social. Their social networks have become richer and denser, and they have become more equitable in whom they interact with. Although multiple factors may be driving this change, at minimum we know the monkeys have become more tolerant of each other. This echoes what we sometimes see in ourselves when communities come together to support each other after natural disasters like tornadoes and floods or events like the September 11, 2001, terrorist attacks. The lessons for managing stress in the office couldn't be clearer, and the challenges for managing these stresses while social distancing through a pandemic couldn't be starker.

This book provides a glimpse of our growing understanding of the structure and function of the human brain, and the ways in which this knowledge can be applied to improve ourselves, our communities, and our businesses. Advances in neurotechnology, combined with sophisticated analytics, offer the potential to know ourselves better and use this knowledge to radically enhance the way we live and the way we work. Although these applications can be potentially abused for greed or power, I'm more optimistic than pessimistic that neuroscience and business can be harmonized to create value for consumers, companies, and society. Indeed, given the challenges of living and working in the 21st century, we're going to need all the help we can get.

Acknowledgments

Writing a book is never easy, but this one was made more pleasurable, and much more doable, with the expert help of Lauren Starkey, Brett LoGiurato, Shannon Berning, and all the great folks at Wharton School Press. Thank you!

My intellectual path has been unusually winding, beginning in anthropology, moving through ethology and psychology, then neuroscience, and on to business. I have been fortunate to have been mentored by many of the most creative and expansive thinkers in these fields, including my undergraduate advisor Alison Richard, my PhD supervisors Dorothy Cheney and Robert Seyfarth, my postdoctoral mentor Paul Glimcher, and Duke neurobiology chair Dale Purves, as well as many other colleagues and friends I have encountered along the way. My work has also been supported by visionary leaders at Duke and Penn, notably former Duke provost Peter Lange, former Wharton dean Geoffrey Garrett, Perelman School of Medicine dean Larry Jameson, Penn School of Arts and Sciences dean Steve Fluharty, and, of course, Penn president Amy Gutmann—who all believe in and promote the interdisciplinary spirit at the heart of this book.

I owe deep gratitude to the postdoctoral scholars, PhD students, master's students, undergraduates, staff, and even high school students who made the lab such an intellectually stimulating, productive, and fun place to work. I am especially indebted to Alli McCoy, Jamie Roitman, Rob Deaner, Stephen Shepherd, Karli Watson, Monica Carlson, Ben Hayden, Sarah Heilbronner, Jeffrey Klein, Becket Ebitz, Steve Chang, Lauren Brent, Noah Snyder-Mackler, Weisong Ong, Yao Jiang, Heidi Steffen, Arjun Ramakrishnan, Sharika KM, Mike Montague, Feng Sheng, Annamarie Huttunen, Sebastien Tremblay,

Camille Testard, Scott Rennie, and Vera Ludwig. You are the real foundations of this book.

I have spent much of the past decade, at Duke and at Wharton, working alongside Zab Johnson, who was associate director of the Duke Institute for Brain Sciences and is currently executive director of the Wharton Neuroscience Initiative. None of this would have been possible without her partnership and willingness to take the leap to join me at Wharton on what at the time was a deeply risky venture.

I thank my family for granting me the space—literally, during the COVID-19 lockdown—to write this book. My three sons, Henry, Zachary, and Tycho, have provided inspiration, confusion, physical challenges, and comic relief along the journey.

Finally, I thank my wife and soul mate Elizabeth Brannon, whom I met on my first monkey-watching expedition in Mexico in 1988. Never could I have imagined we'd end up faculty at Penn—in the same psychology department no less—where we began this intellectual journey together 30 years ago, strolling down Locust Walk to attend seminars with Dorothy and Robert, and eating lunch at Beijing. Juno has replaced Fossey, but otherwise much is the same. I can't wait to see where the next 30 years will lead us.

Notes

1 Alice Fothergill and Seana Lowe, "A Need to Help: Emergent Volunteer Behavior after September 11th," in *Beyond September 11th: An Account of Post-Disaster Research* (Boulder, CO: Natural Hazards Research and Applications Information Center, University of Colorado Boulder, 2003), 293–314; Michael K. Lindell, "Recovery and Reconstruction after Disaster," in *Encyclopedia of Natural Hazards*, ed. Peter Bobrowsky (New York: Springer, 2013), 812–824.

2 Jerome Sallet et al., "Social Network Size Affects Neural Circuits in Macaques," *Science* 334, no. 6056 (2011): 697–700, https://www.researchgate.net/profile /Jerome_Sallet/publication/51769857_Social_Network_Size_Affects_Neural _Circuits_in_Macaques/links/0912f509165f1f1bf0000000.pdf.

3 Adam Galinsky and Maurice Schweitzer, *Friend & Foe: When to Cooperate, When to Compete, and How to Succeed at Both* (New York: Random House, 2015).

4 Galinsky and Schweitzer, 52.

5 Julianne Holt-Lunstad, Timothy B. Smith, and J. Bradley Layton, "Social Relationships and Mortality Risk: A Meta-analytic Review," *PLoS Medicine* 7, no. 7 (2010), https://doi.org/10.1371/journal.pmed.1000316.

6 See Ichiro Kawachi and Lisa F. Berkman, "Social Ties and Mental Health," *Journal of Urban Health: Bulletin of the New York Academy of Medicine* 78, no. 3 (2001): 458–467, https://www.ncbi.nlm.nih.gov/pmc/articles/PMC3455910/pdf /11524_2006_Article_44.pdf.

7 Sarvada Chandra Tiwari, "Loneliness: A Disease?," *Indian Journal of Psychiatry* 55, no. 4 (2013): 320–322, https://www.researchgate.net/publication/259883733 _Loneliness_A_disease.

8 Melissa Harrell and Lauren Barbato, "Great Managers Still Matter: The Evolution of Google's Project Oxygen," *re:Work* (blog), Google, February 27, 2018, https://rework.withgoogle.com/blog/the-evolution-of-project-oxygen/.

9 Leslie Brothers, "The Social Brain: A Project for Integrating Primate Behavior and Neurophysiology in a New Domain," *Concepts in Neuroscience* 1 (1990): 27–51, https://direct.mit.edu/books/book/2431/chapter-abstract/64376/The -Social-Brain-A-Project-for-Integrating-Primate?redirectedFrom=fulltext.

10 Sallet et al., "Social Network Size," 697–700.

11   Uri Hasson and Thalia P. Wheatley, "Brain-to-Brain Dynamical Coupling: A New Framework for the Communication of Social Knowledge," National Institutes of Health (grant proposal), 2017, https://grantome.com/grant/NIH /R01-MH112566-01.

12   Laura Sanders, "Our Brains Sculpt Each Other. So Why Do We Study Them in Isolation?," *Science News*, April 9, 2019, https://www.sciencenews.org/article /brains-sculpt-each-other-social-interactions.

13   V. Heng et al., "Neurological Effects of Moving from an Enriched Environment to Social Isolation in Adult Mice," Society for Neuroscience meeting (2018) Program No. 291.02, https://www.slideshare.net/BARRYSTANLEY2fasd /neurological-effects-of-moving-from-an-enriched-environment-to-social -isolation-in-adult-mice.

14   Sanders, "Our Brains Sculpt Each Other."

15   Miho Nagasaw et al., "Oxytocin-Gaze Positive Loop and the Coevolution of Human-Dog Bonds," *Science* 348, no. 6232 (2015): 333–336, https://science .sciencemag.org/content/348/6232/333.abstract.

16   K. C. Berridge, "Measuring Hedonic Impact in Animals and Infants: Microstructure of Affective Taste Reactivity Patterns," *Neuroscience and Biobehavioral Reviews* 24 (2000): 173–198, https://lsa.umich.edu/psych /research&labs/Berridge/publications/BerridgehedonicimpactNeurosciBiobehv Rev2000.pdf.

17   Spike Jonze, "Ikea Ad," YouTube video, 1:00, https://www.youtube.com/watch?v =TsQXQGaasUg.

18   Clifford Nass and Youngme Moon, "Machines and Mindlessness: Social Responses to Computers," *Journal of Social Issues* 56, no. 1 (2000): 81–103, https://psycnet.apa.org/record/2000-00196-006; Byron Reeves and Clifford Nass, *The Media Equation: How People Treat Computers, Television, and New Media Like Real People and Places* (New York: Cambridge University Press, 1996).

19   Nick Deligiannis, "The Benefits and Downsides of Working in a Flatter Hierarchy," *Silicon Republic* (blog), Sept. 18, 2019, https://www.siliconrepublic .com/advice/flatter-hierarchy-hays-nick-delgiannis.

20   "Servant Leaders: Zingerman's," Greenleaf Center for Servant Leadership, https://www.greenleaf.org/winning-workplaces/profiles-for-success/hospitality /servant-leaders/ (accessed October 22, 2019).

21   Richard Boyatzis, "Neuroscience and Leadership: The Promise of Insights," *Ivey Business Journal*, Jan.–Feb. 2011, https://iveybusinessjournal.com/publication /neuroscience-and-leadership-the-promise-of-insights/.

22   Adrienne Wood, Adam M. Kleinbaum, and Thalia Wheatley, "Cultural Diversity Broadens Social Networks," PsyArXiv, June 3, 2019, https://doi.org/10 .31234/osf.io/qvthk.

23 And Tomas Kellner, "New Power Generation: GE-Alstom Energy Deal Redefines Power Industry in Coming Decades," GE, Nov. 2, 2015, https://www.ge.com/reports/new-power-generation-ge-alstom-energy-deal-redefines-power-industry-coming-decades/.

24 Thomas Gryta and Ted Mann, "GE Powered the American Century—Then It Burned Out," *Wall Street Journal*, Dec. 14, 2018, https://www.wsj.com/articles/ge-powered-the-american-centurythen-it-burned-out-11544796010.

25 Tim Buckley, Kathy Hipple, and Tom Sanzillo, "General Electric Misread the Energy Transition: A Cautionary Tale," Institute for Energy Economics and Financial Analysis, June 2019, https://ieefa.org/wp-content/uploads/2019/06/General-Electric-Misread-the-Energy-Transition_June-2019.pdf.

26 David Keohane, "GE Fined in France for Failing to Create Promised Jobs," *Financial Times*, Feb. 5, 2019, https://www.ft.com/content/c3710368-2955-11e9-88a4-c32129756dd8.

27 Fengtao Shen et al., "Racial Bias in Neural Response for Pain Is Modulated by Minimal Group," *Frontiers in Human Neuroscience*, January 11, 2018, https://www.frontiersin.org/articles/10.3389/fnhum.2017.00661/full.

28 I. Ben-Ami Bartal et al., "Pro-social Behavior in Rats is Modulated by Social Experience," *eLife* 3 (2014): https://doi.org/10.7554/eLife.01385.

29 S. Strang et al., "Impact of Nutrition on Social Decision Making," *Proceedings of the National Academy of Sciences of the United States of America* 114, no. 25 (2017): 6510–6514, https://doi.org/10.1073/pnas.1620245114.

30 R. J. Wurtman et al., "Effects of Normal Meals Rich in Carbohydrates or Proteins on Plasma Tryptophan and Tyrosine Ratios," *American Journal of Clinical Nutrition* 77, no. 1 (2003): 128–132.

31 Ignacio Saez et al., "Dopamine Modulates Egalitarian Behavior in Humans," *Current Biology* 25, no. 7 (2015): 912–919, https://doi.org/10.1016/j.cub.2015.01.071.

32 S. Kühn et al., "Food for Thought: Association Between Dietary Tyrosine and Cognitive Performance in Younger and Older Adults," *Psychological Research* 83, no. 6 (2019): 1097–1106, https://doi.org/10.1007/s00426-017-0957-4.

33 E. M. Swift, "A Reminder of What We Can Be: The 1980 U.S. Olympic Hockey Team," *Sports Illustrated*, Oct. 28, 2014, https://www.si.com/olympics/2014/10/28/reminder-what-we-can-be-1980-us-olympic-hockey-team-si-60.

34 Martine Haas and Mark Mortensen, "The Secrets of Great Teamwork," *Harvard Business Review*, June 2016, https://hbr.org/2016/06/the-secrets-of-great-teamwork.

35 F. Behrens et al., "Physical Synchrony Promotes Cooperative Success in Real-Life Interactions," BioRxiv, October 5, 2019, https://www.biorxiv.org/content/10.1101/792416v1.full.

36 Pam Belluck, "Hearts Beat as One in Daring Ritual," *New York Times*, May 2, 2011, https://www.nytimes.com/2011/05/03/science/03firewalker.html.

37   Suzanne Dikker et al., "Brain-to-Brain Synchrony Tracks Real-World Dynamic
      Group Interactions in the Classroom," *Current Biology* 27 (2017): 1375–1380,
      http://www.psych.nyu.edu/vanbavel/lab/documents/Dikker.etal.2017.CB.pdf.

38   Takahiko Koike et al., "What Makes Eye Contact Special? Neural Substrates of
      On-line Mutual Eye-Gaze: A Hyperscanning fMRI Study," *eNeuro* 6, no. 1
      (2019): https://www.eneuro.org/content/6/1/ENEURO.0284-18.2019.

39   See Dikker et al., "Brain-to-Brain Synchrony"; and Lydia Denworth,
      "Hyperscans Show How Brains Synch as People Interact," *Scientific American*,
      Apr. 10, 2019, https://www.scientificamerican.com/article/hyperscans-show
      -how-brains-sync-as-people-interact/.

40   Y. Jiang and M. L. Platt, "Oxytocin and Vasopressin Flatten Dominance
      Hierarchy and Enhance Behavioral Synchrony in Part via Anterior Cingulate
      Cortex," *Scientific Reports* 8 (2018): https://doi.org/10.1038/s41598-018-25607-1.

41   Y. Yeshurun et al., "Same Story, Different Story: The Neural Representation of
      Interpretive Frameworks," *Psychological Science* 28, no. 3 (2017): 307–319,
      https://doi.org/10.1177/0956797616682029.

42   Chris Voss, *Never Split the Difference: Negotiating as If Your Life Depended on It*
      (New York: Harper Business, 2016).

43   Libby Kane, "Why Every New Employee at a Billion-Dollar Glasses Brand Gets
      Kerouac and Pretzels as a Welcome Gift," *Business Insider*, Apr. 14, 2017, https://
      www.businessinsider.com/how-warby-parker-builds-company-culture-2017-4.

44   Jay J. Van Bavel et al., "The Neuroscience of Leading Effective Teams,"
      NeuroLeadership Journal 7 (2018): http://www.psych.nyu.edu/vanbavel/lab
      /documents/VanBavel.etal.2018.NL.pdf.

45   P. Molenberghs and W. R. Louis, "Insights from fMRI Studies into Ingroup
      Bias," *Frontiers in Psychology* 9 (2018): https://doi.org/10.3389/fpsyg.2018.01868.

46   Ben Rowen, "Chasing the 'Holy Grail' of Baseball Performance," *The Atlantic*,
      July–Aug. 2018, https://www.theatlantic.com/magazine/archive/2018/07/finding
      -the-formula-for-team-chemistry/561722/.

47   Scott A. Brave, R. Andrew Butters, and Kevin Roberts, "In Search of David
      Ross," MIT Sloan Sports Analytics Conference, 2017, http://www
      .sloansportsconference.com/wp-content/uploads/2017/02/1636.pdf.

48   Jared Diamond, "Baseball Tackles Workplace Mystery: How to Build Team
      Chemistry?," *Wall Street Journal*, July 12, 2017, https://www.wsj.com/articles
      /baseball-tackles-workplace-mystery-how-to-build-team-chemistry-1499875993.

49   Russell A. Carleton, "Baseball Therapy: Can't Buy Me Chemistry?," Baseball
      Prospectus, Feb. 26, 2013, https://www.baseballprospectus.com/news/article
      /19704/baseball-therapy-cant-buy-me-chemistry/.

50   James K. Harter, Frank L. Schmidt, and Corey L. M. Keyes, "Wellbeing in the
      Workplace and Its Relationship to Business Outcomes," Gallup, http://media
      .gallup.com/documents/whitePaper--Well-BeingInTheWorkplace.pdf.

51 Martine Haas, "Leading Virtual Teams: Overcoming Key Challenges"(Nano Tool), Wharton@Work, June 2020, https://execed.wharton.upenn.edu/thought -leadership/wharton-at-work/2020/06/leading-virtual-teams/.

52 Albert Mehrabian, *Silent Messages*, 1st ed. (Belmont, CA: Wadsworth, 1971); J. Cesario and E. T. Higgins, "Making Message Recipients 'Feel Right': How Nonverbal Cues Can Increase Persuasion," *Psychological Science* 19, no. 5 (2008): 415–420, https://doi.org/10.1111/j.1467-9280.2008.02102.x.

53 F. Sheng and S. Han, "Manipulations of Cognitive Strategies and Intergroup Relationships Reduce the Racial Bias in Empathic Neural Responses," *NeuroImage* 61, no. 4 (2012): 786–797, https://doi.org/10.1016/j.neuroimage.2012 .04.028.

54 Bob Graham et al., *Deep Water: The Gulf Oil Disaster and the Future of Offshore Drilling* (report to the President), National Commission on the BP Deepwater Horizon Oil Spill and Offshore Drilling, January 2011, https://www.govinfo.gov /content/pkg/GPO-OILCOMMISSION/pdf/GPO-OILCOMMISSION.pdf.

55 Elizabeth Shogren, "BP: A Textbook Example of How Not to Handle PR," National Public Radio, Apr. 21, 2011, https://www.npr.org/2011/04/21/135575238 /bp-a-textbook-example-of-how-not-to-handle-pr.

56 Tom Bergin and Francis Kerry, "BP CEO Apologizes for 'Thoughtless' Oil Spill Comment," Reuters, June 2, 2010, https://www.reuters.com/article/us-oil-spill -bp-apology/bp-ceo-apologizes-for-thoughtless-oil-spill-comment -idUSTRE6515NQ20100602.

57 Yeshurun et al., "Same Story, Different Story."

58 Yeshurun et al., "Same Story, Different Story," 318.

59 Stella Collins, *Neuroscience for Learning and Development: How to Apply Neuroscience and Psychology for Improved Learning and Training*, 2nd ed. (London: Kogan Page, 2019).

60 Robert Cialdini, *Pre-suasion: A Revolutionary Way to Influence and Persuade* (New York: Simon & Schuster, 2018).

61 Cialdini, *Pre-suasion*.

62 *2017 Work and Well-Being Survey*, American Psychological Association, http://www.apaexcellence.org/assets/general/2017-work-and-wellbeing-survey -results.pdf?_ga=2.30624635.552121507.1583180964-1805362551.1580758482 (accessed December 4, 2019).

63 Yoona Kang et al., "Effects of Self-Transcendence on Neural Responses to Persuasive Messages and Health Behavior Change," *Proceedings of the National Academy of Sciences*, September 17, 2018, https://www.pnas.org/content/115/40 /9974.

64 Frank J. Berinieri et al., "Interactional Synchrony and Rapport: Measuring Synchrony in Displays Devoid of Sound and Facial Affect," *Personality and Social Psychology Bulletin* 20, no. 3 (1994): 303–311, https://www.researchgate

.net/publication/247746617_Interactional_Synchrony_and_Rapport
_Measuring_Synchrony_in_Displays_Devoid_of_Sound_and_Facial_Affect.

65 Tanya L. Chartrand and John A. Bargh, "The Chameleon Effect: The Perception-
    Behavior Link and Social Interaction," *Journal of Personality and Social
    Psychology* 76, no. 6 (1999): 893–910, https://psycnet.apa.org/record/1999-05479
    -002.

66 Uri Hasson et al., "Intersubject Synchronization of Cortical Activity during
    Natural Vision," *Science* 303, no. 5664 (2004): 1634–1640, https://science
    .sciencemag.org/content/303/5664/1634.

67 Sam Barnett and Moran Cerf, "A Ticket for Your Thoughts: Method for
    Predicting Content Recall and Sales Using Neural Similarity of Moviegoers,"
    Journal of Consumer Research 44, no. 1 (2017): 160–181, https://www
    .researchgate.net/publication/317767548_A_Ticket_for_Your_Thoughts
    _Method_for_Predicting_Content_Recall_and_Sales_Using_Neural
    _Similarity_of_Moviegoers.

68 Collins, *Neuroscience for Learning and Development*.

69 Chip Heath and Dan Heath, *Made to Stick: Why Some Ideas Survive and Others
    Die* (New York: Random House, 2007).

70 "Hearing Metaphors Activates Sensory Brain Regions," Emory News Center,
    Feb. 7, 2012, https://news.emory.edu/stories/2012/02/metaphor_brain_imaging/.

71 Julio González et al., "Reading Cinnamon Activates Olfactory Brain Regions,"
    NeuroImage 32, no. 2 (2006): 906–912, https://www.researchgate.net/publication
    /7130495_Reading_cinnamon_activates_olfactory_brain_regions.

72 Jonah Berger, *Contagious: Why Things Catch On* (New York: Simon & Schuster,
    2016), 123.

73 "Putting a Face to a Name: The Art of Motivating Employees," Knowledge@
    Wharton, Feb. 17, 2010, https://knowledge.wharton.upenn.edu/article/putting-a
    -face-to-a-name-the-art-of-motivating-employees/.

74 Alex B. Van Zant and Jonah Berger, "How the Voice Persuades," *Journal of
    Personality and Social Psychology* 118, no. 4 (2020): 661–682, https://psycnet.apa
    .org/buy/2019-31309-001.

75 Tim Herrera, "How to—Literally—Sound More Confident and Persuasive,"
    Smarter Living, *New York Times*, Nov. 10, 2019, https://www.nytimes.com/2019
    /11/10/smarter-living/how-to-sound-more-confident-persuasive.html.

76 "Mastering the Art of Effective Communication: What Big Data Can Tell Us,"
    Knowledge@Wharton, May 5, 2016, https://knowledge.wharton.upenn.edu
    /article/the-science-of-effective-communication/.

77 *2018 Workplace Learning Report: The Rise and Responsibility of Talent Development
    in the New Labor Market*, LinkedIn Learning, https://learning.linkedin.com
    /resources/workplace-learning-report-2018 (accessed January 6, 2020).

78 Victor Lipman, "65% of Employees Want More Feedback (So Why Don't They Get It?)," *Forbes*, Aug. 8, 2016, https://www.forbes.com/sites/victorlipman/2016/08/08/65-of-employees-want-more-feedback-so-why-dont-they-get-it/#6f59b3f3914a; "An Imperfect Test: The Problem with Job Performance Appraisals," Knowledge@Wharton, May 23, 2016, https://knowledge.wharton.upenn.edu/article/the-problem-with-job-performance-appraisals/.

79 Martin Bressler and Clarence Woodrow Von Bergen, "The Sandwich Feedback Method: Not Very Tasty," *Journal of Behavioral Studies in Business*, Jan. 2014, https://www.researchgate.net/publication/281034931_The_Sandwich_Feedback_Method_not_very_tasty.

80 Shalini Ramachandran and Joe Flint, "At Netflix, Radical Transparency and Blunt Firings Unsettle the Ranks," *Wall Street Journal*, Oct. 25, 2018, https://www.wsj.com/articles/at-netflix-radical-transparency-and-blunt-firings-unsettle-the-ranks-1540497174.

81 David Rock, Beth Jones, and Chris Weller, "The Hidden Leverage of Feedback," *Psychology Today*, Jan. 7, 2019, https://www.psychologytoday.com/us/blog/your-brain-work/201901/the-hidden-leverage-feedback.

82 ———, "Using Neuroscience to Make Feedback Work and Feel Better," *Strategy+Business*, Aug. 27, 2018, https://www.strategy-business.com/article/Using-Neuroscience-to-Make-Feedback-Work-and-Feel-Better?gko=6aca6.

83 Adam Bryant, "Google's Quest to Build a Better Boss," *New York Times*, Mar. 12, 2011, https://www.nytimes.com/2011/03/13/business/13hire.html.

84 A. J. Harbinger, "7 Things Everyone Should Know about the Art of Eye Contact," *Art of Charm* (blog), *Business Insider*, May 14, 2015, https://www.businessinsider.com/the-power-of-eye-contact-2015-5.

85 Tim Higgins and Mike Spector, "Tesla Blames Driver in Fatal Car Crash," *Wall Street Journal*, Apr. 11, 2018, https://www.wsj.com/articles/tesla-blames-driver-in-fatal-car-crash-1523487100.

86 Kevin N. Ochsner and James J. Gross, "The Cognitive Control of Emotion," *Trends in Cognitive Psychology* 9, no. 5 (2005): 242–249, https://www.ncbi.nlm.nih.gov/pubmed/15866151.

87 Matthew D. Lieberman et al., "Putting Feelings into Words: Affect Labeling Disrupts Amygdala Activity in Response to Affective Stimuli," *Psychological Science* 18, no. 5 (2007): 421–428, https://www.ncbi.nlm.nih.gov/pubmed/17576282.

88 Dale Archer, "ADHD: The Entrepreneur's Superpower," *Forbes*, May 14, 2014, https://www.forbes.com/sites/dalearcher/2014/05/14/adhd-the-entrepreneurs-superpower/#2fc2295759e9; Joe De Sena, "I'm a CEO with ADHD and It's My Biggest Strength. Here's Why," *Business Insider*, Oct. 8, 2019, https://www.businessinsider.com/im-ceo-with-adhd-its-my-biggest-strength-heres-why-2019-10.

89 Franco Fiordelisis et al., "Creative Corporate Culture and Innovation" (Finance Working Paper No. 578/2018, European Corporate Governance Institute, Nov. 2018), https://ecgi.global/sites/default/files/working_papers/documents/fin alfiordelisirenneboogriccilopes.pdf.

90 Forrester Consulting, "The Creative Dividend: How Creativity Impacts Business Results," Forrester Research Inc., Aug. 2014, https://landing.adobe.com/dam /downloads/whitepapers/55563.en.creative-dividends.pdf.

91 Amy Novotney, "Despite What You've Been Told, You're Not 'Left-Brained' or 'Right-Brained,'" *The Guardian*, Nov. 16, 2013, https://www.theguardian.com /commentisfree/2013/nov/16/left-right-brain-distinction-myth.

92 Roger Beaty et al., "Robust Prediction of Individual Creative Ability from Brain Functional Connectivity," *Proceedings of the National Academy of Sciences* 115, no. 5 (2018): 1087–1092, https://www.pnas.org/content/115/5/1087.

93 Marcus E. Raichle et al., "A Default Mode of Brain Function," *Proceedings of the National Academy of Sciences* 98, no. 2 (2001): 676–682, https://www.pnas.org /content/98/2/676.

94 David L. Barack, Steven W. C. Chang, and Michael L. Platt, "Posterior Cingulate Neurons Dynamically Signal Decisions to Disengage during Foraging," *Neuron* 96 (2017): 339–347, https://www.cell.com/neuron/pdfExtended/S0896 -6273(17)30917-0.

95 Benjamin Y. Hayden et al., "Posterior Cingulate Cortex Mediates Outcome-Contingent Allocation of Behavior," *Neuron* 60, no. 1 (2008): 19–25, https:// www.ncbi.nlm.nih.gov/pubmed/18940585.

96 Sarah R. Heilbronner, Benjamin Y. Hayden, and Michael L. Platt, "Decision Salience Signals in Posterior Cingulate Cortex," *Frontiers in Neuroscience* 5 (2011): 55, https://www.ncbi.nlm.nih.gov/pmc/articles/PMC3082768/.

97 J. P. Guilford, "The Structure of Intellect," *Psychological Bulletin* 53, no. 4 (1956): 267–293.

98 Courtney Turrin et al., "Social Resource Foraging Is Guided by the Principles of the Marginal Value Theorem," *Scientific Reports* 7, no. 11274 (2017), https:// www.nature.com/articles/s41598-017-11763-3.

99 Eric L. Charnov, "Optimal Foraging, the Marginal Value Theorem," *Theoretical Population Biology* 9, no. 2 (1976): 129–136, https://www.sciencedirect.com /science/article/pii/004058097690040X.

100 Barack, Chang, and Platt, "Posterior Cingulate Neurons."

101 Alejandro López-Cruz et al., "Parallel Multimodal Circuits Control an Innate Foraging Behavior," *Neuron* 102 (2019): 407–419, https://www.cell.com/neuron /pdfExtended/S0896-6273(19)30080-7.

102 Nicolas Dallière et al., "*Caenorhabditis elegans* Feeding Behavior," *Oxford Research Encyclopedias*, June 2017, https://oxfordre.com/neuroscience/view/10 .1093/acrefore/9780190264086.001.0001/acrefore-9780190264086-e-190.

103 Matthijs Dekker, "Creativity through the Eyes: Arousal and the Prediction of Creative Task Performance by Locus Coeruleus-norepinephrine Modes" (master's thesis, Tilburg University, 2017), http://arno.uvt.nl/show.cgi?fid =142462.

104 Bryant J. Kongkees and Lorenza S. Colzato, "Spontaneous Eye Blink Rate as Predictor of Dopamine-Related Cognitive Function: A Review," *Neuroscience and Biobehavioral Reviews* 71 (Dec. 2016): 58–82, https://www.sciencedirect .com/science/article/pii/S0149763416302846.

105 Thomas T. Hills, Peter M. Todd, and Robert L. Goldstone, "Search in External and Internal Spaces: Evidence for Generalized Cognitive Search Processes," *Psychological Science*, Aug. 1, 2008, https://journals.sagepub.com/doi/full/10 .1111/j.1467-9280.2008.02160.x.

106 Thierry Malleret and Christopher Maxwell, "Enhance Decision Making and Problem Solving by Walking" (Nano Tool), Wharton@Work, Sept. 2018, https://executiveeducation.wharton.upenn.edu/thought-leadership/wharton-at -work/2018/09/decision-making-and-problem-solving-by-walking/.

107 Marily Oppezzo and Daniel L. Schwartz, "Give Your Ideas Some Legs: The Positive Effect of Walking on Creative Thinking," *Journal of Experimental Psychology: Learning, Memory, and Cognition* 40, no. 4 (2014): 1142–1152, https://psycnet.apa.org/record/2014-14435-001.

108 Michael Platt, "Innovative Thinking: Using Neuroscience to Get Out-of-the-Box Ideas" (Nano Tool), Wharton@Work, Oct. 2017, https://executiveeducation .wharton.upenn.edu/thought-leadership/wharton-at-work/2017/10/innovative -thinking-using-neuroscience/.

109 Siobhan Smith, "The Companies That Encourage Staff to Socialise with Each Other," inews, Feb. 3, 2017, https://inews.co.uk/inews-lifestyle/work/companies -encourage-staff-socialise-work-office-529616.

110 Shana Lebowitz, "Salesforce CEO Marc Benioff Relies on the Same Zen Buddhist Concept That Propelled Steve Jobs to Success," *Business Insider*, Aug. 2016, https://www.businessinsider.com/salesforce-marc-benioff-beginners-mind-2016-8.

111 Charly Kleissner, "A Year of Impact—Personal Reflections" (web page), ImpactAssets, https://www.impactassets.org/a-year-of-impact-personal -reflections (accessed January 22, 2020).

112 Ginamarie Scott, Lyle E. Leritz, and Michael D. Mumford, "The Effectiveness of Creativity Training," *Creativity Research Journal* 16, no. 4 (2004): 361–388, https://www.researchgate.net/publication/272177953_The_Effectiveness_of _Creativity_Training_A_Quantitative_Review.

113 David Tanner, *Igniting Innovation through the Power of Creative Thinking* (Myers House LLC, 2008).

114 "ShipIt: 24 Hours to Innovate. It's Like 20% Time. On Steroids" (web page), Atlassian, https://www.atlassian.com/company/shipit (accessed February 4, 2020).

115 Joel A. Lopata, Elizabeth A. Nowicki, and Marc F. Joanisse, "Creativity as a Distinct Trainable Mental State: An EEG Study of Musical Improvisation," *Neuropsychologia* 99 (May 2017): 246–258, https://www.sciencedirect.com/science/article/abs/pii/S0028393217300994.

116 "Creativity Is a State of Mind That Can Be Trained," Neuroscience News, Apr. 21, 2018, https://neurosciencenews.com/creativity-trained-8854/.

117 Scott Barry Kaufman and Elliot S. Paul, "Creativity and Schizophrenia Spectrum Disorders across the Arts and Sciences," *Frontiers in Psychology* 5 (2014): 1145, https://www.ncbi.nlm.nih.gov/pmc/articles/PMC4217346/.

118 "Is ADHD an Advantage for Nomadic Tribesmen?," Science Daily, June 10, 2008, https://www.sciencedaily.com/releases/2008/06/080609195604.htm.

119 Hannah Nichols, "Is ADHD Genetic? Everything You Need to Know," Medical News Today, June 28, 2019, https://www.medicalnewstoday.com/articles/325594.

120 Daniel Pink, *When: The Scientific Secrets of Perfect Timing* (New York: Riverhead Books, 2018).

121 A. C. Hafenbrack, Z. Kinias, and S. G. Barsade, "Debiasing the Mind Through Meditation: Mindfulness and the Sunk-Cost Bias," *Psychological Science* 25, no. 2 (2014): 369–376, https://doi.org/10.1177/0956797613503853.

122 Benjamin de Hass et al., "Perception and Processing of Faces in the Human Brain Is Tuned to Typical Feature Locations," *Journal of Neuroscience* 36, no. 6 (Sept. 2016): 9289–9302, https://www.ncbi.nlm.nih.gov/pmc/articles/PMC5013182/.

123 Benjamin W. Tatler et al., "Yarbus, Eye Movements, and Vision," *Iperception* 1, no. 1 (2010): 7–27, https://www.ncbi.nlm.nih.gov/pmc/articles/PMC3563050/.

124 Gregory Ciotti, "7 Marketing Lessons from Eye-Tracking Studies" (blog), Neil Patel, https://neilpatel.com/blog/eye-tracking-studies/ (accessed February 12, 2020).

125 Kara Pernice, "F-Shaped Pattern of Reading on the Web: Misunderstood, but Still Relevant (Even on Mobile)," Nielsen Norman Group, Nov. 12, 2017, https://www.nngroup.com/articles/f-shaped-pattern-reading-web-content/.

126 P. Christiaan Klinck, Pia Jentgens, and Jeannette A. M. Lorteije, "Priority Maps Explain the Roles of Value, Attention, and Salience in Goal-Oriented Behavior," *Journal of Neuroscience* 34, no. 42 (Oct. 2014): 13867–13869, https://www.jneurosci.org/content/34/42/13867.

127 Jianming Zeng et al., "Predicting the Behavioural Tendency of Loss Aversion," *Scientific Reports* 9 (2019): 5024, https://www.ncbi.nlm.nih.gov/pmc/articles/PMC6430803/.

128 Feng Sheng et al., "Decomposing Loss Aversion from Gaze Allocation and Pupil Dilation," *Proceedings of the National Academy of Sciences* 117, no. 21 (May 2020): https://www.biorxiv.org/content/10.1101/2020.02.27.967711v2.

129   Cary Frydman and Antonia Rangel, "Debiasing the Disposition Effect by Reducing the Saliency of Information about a Stock's Purchase Price," *Journal of Economic Behavior & Organization* 107, pt. B (Nov. 2014): 541–552, https://www.ncbi.nlm.nih.gov/pmc/articles/PMC4357845/.

130   Ian Krajbich et al., "The Attentional Drift-Diffusion Model Extends to Simple Purchasing Decisions," *Frontiers in Psychology* 3 (2012): 193, https://www.ncbi.nlm.nih.gov/pmc/articles/PMC3374478/.

131   Apoorva Rajiv Madipakkam et al., "The Influence of Gaze Direction on Food Preferences," *Scientific Reports* 9 (2019): https://www.nature.com/articles/s41598-019-41815-9.

132   Arani Roy, Stephen V. Shepherd, and Michael L. Platt, "Reversible Inactivation of pSTS Suppresses Social Gaze Following in the Macaque (*Macaca mulatta*)," *Social Cognitive and Affective Neuroscience* 9, no. 2 (Feb. 2014): 209–217, https://academic.oup.com/scan/article/9/2/209/1620877?view=extract.

133   Zhongqiang Sun et al., "Incidental Learning of Group Trust: Predictive Gaze Cue Matters," *Scientific Reports* 10 (2020): 7789, https://www.nature.com/articles/s41598-020-64719-5.

134   Peter Cappelli, "Your Approach to Hiring Is All Wrong," *Harvard Business Review*, May–June 2019, https://hbr.org/2019/05/recruiting.

135   Sheena S. Iyengar and Mark R. Lepper, "When Choice Is Demotivating: Can One Desire Too Much of a Good Thing?," *Journal of Personality and Social Psychology* 79, no. 6 (2000): 995–1006, https://www.researchgate.net/profile/Mark_Lepper/publication/12189991_When_Choice_is_Demotivating_Can_One_Desire_Too__Much_of_a_Good_Thing/links/56107d7d08ae6b29b49c75fa/When-Choice-is-Demotivating-Can-One-Desire-Too-Much-of-a-Good-Thing.pdf.

136   Benjamin Scheibehenne, Rainer Greifeneder, and Peter M. Todd, "Can There Ever Be Too Many Options?," *Journal of Consumer Research* 37, no. 3 (Oct. 2010): 409–425, https://academic.oup.com/jcr/article-abstract/37/3/409/1827647; Daniel Mochon, "Single-Option Aversion," *Journal of Consumer Research* 40, no. 3 (Oct. 2013): 555–566, https://academic.oup.com/jcr/articleabstract/40/3/555/2379775.

137   Maria Cohut, "Choice Overload: Why Decision-Making Can Be So Hard," *Medical News Today*, Oct. 3, 2018, https://www.medicalnewstoday.com/articles/323243.php#1.

138   "Ebbinghaus Illusion," Illusions Index, https://www.illusionsindex.org/ir/ebbinghaus-illusion (accessed February 28, 2020).

139   De Martino et al., "Frames, Biases, and Rational Decision-Making in the Human Brain," *Science* 313, no. 5787 (2006): 684–687.

140   Derek Thompson, "More Is More: Why the Paradox of Choice Might Be a Myth," *The Atlantic*, Aug. 9, 2013, https://www.theatlantic.com/business/archive/2013/08/more-is-more-why-the-paradox-of-choice-might-be-a-myth/278658/.

141 Brittany Paris, "The Decoy Effect and Investors' Stock Preferences" (honors theses and capstones, University of New Hampshire, 2012), http://scholars.unh.edu/cgi/viewcontent.cgi?article=1011&context=honors.

142 Terry Connolly, Jochen Reb, and Edgar E. Kausel, "Regret Saliency and Accountability in the Decoy Effect," *Judgment and Decision Making* 8, no. 2 (2013): 136–149, https://ink.library.smu.edu.sg/cgi/viewcontent.cgi?article =4632&context=lkcsb_research.

143 Robyn A. Berkley and David M. Kaplan, *Strategic Training and Development* (Newbury Park, CA: SAGE Publications, 2019), 93, https://www.google.com /books/edition/Strategic_Training_and_Development/1MGeDwAAQBAJ?hl =en&gbpv=1&dq=Strategic+Training+and+Development&printsec=frontcover.

144 Harold Pashler et al., "Learning Styles: Concepts and Evidence," *Psychological Science in the Public Interest* 9, no. 3 (December 2008): 105–119, https://www .jstor.org/stable/20697325?seq=1.

145 James J. Choi et al., "Reinforcement Learning and Savings Behavior," *Journal of Finance* 64, no. 6 (Dec. 2009): 2515–2534, https://www.ncbi.nlm.nih.gov/pmc /articles/PMC2845178/.

146 Jill Rosen, "Johns Hopkins Finds Training Exercise That Boosts Brain Power," news release, Johns Hopkins University, Oct. 17, 2017, https://releases.jhu.edu /2017/10/17/johns-hopkins-finds-training-exercise-that-boosts-brain-power/.

147 Joseph W. Kable et al., "No Effect of Commercial Cognitive Training on Brain Activity, Choice Behavior, or Cognitive Performance," *Journal of Neuroscience* 37, no. 31 (Aug. 2017): 7390–7402, https://www.jneurosci.org/content/37/31 /7390.

148 Adam Bryant, "In Head-Hunting, Big Data May Not Be Such a Big Deal," *New York Times*, June 19, 2013, https://www.nytimes.com/2013/06/20/business/in -head-hunting-big-data-may-not-be-such-a-big-deal.html?_r=0.

149 Joshua D. Berke and Steven E. Hyman, "Addiction, Dopamine, and the Molecular Mechanisms of Memory," *Neuron* 25, no. 3 (Mar. 2000): 515–532, https://www.sciencedirect.com/science/article/pii/S0896627300810569.

150 Steven E. Hyman and Robert C. Malenka, "Addiction and the Brain: The Neurobiology of Compulsion and Its Persistence," *Nature Reviews Neuroscience* 2 (Oct. 2001): 695–703, https://www.nature.com/articles/35094560/.

151 Joseph W. Kable and Paul W. Glimcher, "The Neurobiology of Decision: Consensus and Controversy," *Neuron* 63, no. 6 (Sept. 2009): 733–745, https:// www.sciencedirect.com/science/article/pii/S0896627309006813.

152 Alain Dagher and Trevor W. Robbins, "Personality, Addiction, Dopamine: Insights from Parkinson's Disease," *Neuron* 61, no. 4 (Feb. 2009): 502–510, https://www.sciencedirect.com/science/article/pii/S089662730900124X.

153 Doron Merims and Nir Giladi, "Dopamine Dysregulation System, Addiction, and Behavioral Changes in Parkinson's Disease," *Parkinsonism and Related*

Disorders 14, no. 4 (May 2008): 273–280, https://www.sciencedirect.com/science /article/abs/pii/S1353802007002088.

154 A. Ross Otto, Stephen M. Fleming, and Paul W. Glimcher, "Unexpected but Incidental Positive Outcomes Predict Real-World Gambling," *Psychological Science* 27, no. 3 (Mar. 2016): 299–311, https://www.ncbi.nlm.nih.gov/pubmed /26796614.

155 Karl Engelking, "There's a Happy App for That," *Discover*, Nov. 26, 2014, https://www.discovermagazine.com/mind/theres-a-happy-app-for-that.

156 Yuan Chang Leong et al., "Dynamic Interaction between Reinforcement Learning and Attention in Multidimensional Environments," *Neuron* 93, no. 2 (Jan. 2017): 451–463, https://www.sciencedirect.com/science/article/pii /S089662731631039X.

157 Carla Fried, "Vacation Mindset: How Weekends Can Be More Refreshing," *UCLA Anderson Review*, Feb. 20, 2019, https://www.anderson.ucla.edu/faculty -and-research/anderson-review/vacation-mindset.

158 Adam M. Grant and Francesca Gino, "A Little Thanks Goes a Long Way: Explaining Why Gratitude Expressions Motivate Prosocial Behavior," *Journal of Personality and Social Psychology* 98, no. 6 (2010): 946–955, https://psycnet.apa .org/record/2010-09990-007.

159 R. Wagner and J. K. Harter, *12: The Elements of Great Managing* (New York: Gallup Press, 2006).

160 Kerry Roberts Gibson et al., "The Little Things That Make Employees Feel Appreciated," *Harvard Business Review*, January 23, 2020, https://hbr.org/2020 /01/the-little-things-that-make-employees-feel-appreciated.

161 Michael L. Platt and Ben Hayden, "Learning: Not Just the Facts, Ma'am, but the Counterfactuals as Well," *PLoS Biology* 9, no. 6 (June 2011), https://journals.plos .org/plosbiology/article?id=10.1371/journal.pbio.1001092.

162 Benjamin Y. Hayden and Michael L. Platt, "Gambling for Gatorade: Risk-Sensitive Decision Making for Fluid Rewards in Humans," *Animal Cognition* 12, no. 1 (Jan. 2009): 201–2017, https://www.ncbi.nlm.nih.gov/pmc/articles /PMC2683409/.

163 For example, Erie D. Boorman, Timothy E. Behrens, and Matthew F. Rushworth, "Counterfactual Choice and Learning in a Neural Network Centered on Human Lateral Frontopolar Cortex," *PLoS Biology*, June 28, 2011, https://journals.plos.org/plosbiology/article?id=10.1371/journal.pbio.1001093.

164 Angela Sirigu and Jean-René Duhamel, "Reward and Decision Processes in the Brains of Humans and Non-human Primates," *Dialogues in Clinical Neuroscience* 18, no. 1 (Mar. 2016): 45–53, https://www.ncbi.nlm.nih.gov/pmc /articles/PMC4826770/.

165 R. Becket Ebitz and Michael L. Platt, "Neuronal Activity in Primate Dorsal Anterior Cingulate Cortex Signals Task Conflict and Predicts Adjustments in

Pupil-Linked Arousal," *Neuron* 85, no. 3 (Feb. 2015): 628–640, https://www
.sciencedirect.com/science/article/pii/S0896627314011623.

166 Charline Uhr, Steffen Meyer, and Andreas Hackethal, "Smoking Hot Portfolios?
Overtrading from Self-Control Failure" (SAFE Working Paper No. 245, Sept.
2019), https://papers.ssrn.com/sol3/papers.cfm?abstract_id=3347625.

167 "'Counterfactual' Thinkers Are More Motivated and Analytical, Study
Suggests," Science Daily, Feb. 9, 2010, https://www.sciencedaily.com/releases
/2010/02/100209100800.htm.

168 Xiaosi Gu et al., "Cognitive Strategies Regulate Fictive, but not Reward
Prediction Error Signals in a Sequential Investment Task," *Human Brain
Mapping* 35, no. 8 (Aug. 2014): 3738–3749, https://www.ncbi.nlm.nih.gov/pmc
/articles/PMC4105325/.

169 Peter Sokol-Hessner et al., "Thinking Like a Trader Selectively Reduces
Individuals' Loss Aversion," *Proceedings of the National Academy of Sciences*
106, no. 13 (2009): 5035–5040, https://www.pnas.org/content/106/13/5035.

170 Xiaomo Chen and Veit Stuphorn, "Inactivation of Medial Frontal Cortex
Changes Risk Preference," *Current Biology* 28, no. 19 (Oct. 2018): 3114–3122,
https://www.cell.com/current-biology/fulltext/S0960-9822(18)30942-4.

171 "How Companies Are Increasing Neurodiversity in the Workplace,"
Knowledge@Wharton, Mar. 28, 2019, https://knowledge.wharton.upenn.edu
/article/autism-employment/.

172 Isobel Asher Hamilton, "Elon Musk Says He's Tested His Brain Microchip on
Monkeys, and It Enabled One to Control a Computer with Its Mind," *Business
Insider*, July 17, 2019, https://www.businessinsider.com/elon-musk-neuralink
-brain-microchip-tested-on-monkeys-2019-7.

173 Justin Martin and Fiery Cushman, "When We Don't Blame People for Their Bad
Deeds," *Harvard Business Review*, Feb. 16, 2016, https://hbr.org/2016/02/when
-we-dont-blame-people-for-their-bad-deeds.

174 Wi Hoon Jung et al., "Moral Competence and Brain Connectivity: A Resting-
State fMRI Study," *Neuroimage* 141 (Nov. 2016): 408–415, https://www.ncbi.nlm
.nih.gov/pmc/articles/PMC5028200/.

175 Gideon Nave et al., "Musical Preferences Predict Personality: Evidence from
Active Listening and Facebook Likes," *Psychological Science*, May 2018,
https://www.researchgate.net/publication/322506461_Musical_Preferences
_Predict_Personality_Evidence_from_Active_Listening_and_Facebook_Likes.

176 Alexander Genevsky and Brian Knutson, "Neural Affective Mechanisms Predict
Market-Level Microlending," *Psychological Science* 26, no. 9 (Sept. 2015):
1411–1422, https://www.ncbi.nlm.nih.gov/pmc/articles/PMC4570982/.

177 Emily B. Falk et al., "Functional Brain Imaging Predicts Public Health
Campaign Success," *Social Cognitive and Affective Neuroscience* 11, no. 2
(Feb. 2016): 204–214, https://www.ncbi.nlm.nih.gov/pmc/articles/PMC4733336/.

178 Yoona Kang et al., "Effects of Self-Transcendence on Neural Responses to Persuasive Messages and Health Behavior Change," *Proceedings of the National Academy of Sciences* 115, no. 40 (Sept. 2018): 9974–9979, https://www.pnas.org /content/115/40/9974.

179 Christian Hasenoehrl, Melissa Swift, and Juliana Barela, "How to Hire 5000 People . . . in a Day," Korn Ferry Insights, https://www.kornferry.com/insights /articles/walmart-hiring-coronavirus-rpo (accessed March 9, 2020).

180 CareerBuilder, "Nearly Three in Four Employers Affected by a Bad Hire, According to a Recent CareerBuilder Survey," press release, December 7, 2017, http://press.careerbuilder.com/2017-12-07-Nearly-Three-in-Four-Employers -Affected-by-a-Bad-Hire-According-to-a-Recent-CareerBuilder-Survey.

181 "Data & Statistics on Autism Spectrum Disorder," Centers for Disease Control and Prevention, last reviewed March 25, 2020, https://www.cdc.gov/ncbddd /autism/data.html.

182 Nicole Lyn Pesce, "Most College Grads with Autism Can't Find Jobs. This Group Is Fixing That," Market Watch, Apr. 2, 2019, https://www.marketwatch.com /story/most-college-grads-with-autism-cant-find-jobs-this-group-is-fixing-that -2017-04-10-5881421.

183 Eric Van Gieson, "Measuring Biological Aptitude (MBA)," Defense Advanced Research Projects Agency, https://www.darpa.mil/program/measuring -biological-aptitude (accessed March 9, 2020).

184 Herbert Simon, "Bounded Rationality and Organizational Learning," *Organization Science* 2, no. 1 (1991): 125–134, https://pubsonline.informs.org/doi/10 .1287/orsc.2.1.125.

185 "2017 Work and Well-Being Survey," American Psychological Association, http://www.apaexcellence.org/assets/general/2017-work-and-wellbeing-survey -results.pdf?_ga=2.119676813.429993371.1581349388-1814347604.1566408625 (accessed March 9 2020).

Index

accuracy, 57–58, 68, 69
ADHD. *see* attention-deficit/
    hyperactivity disorder
Advertising Research Foundation, 96
aging, 73
Alstom, 9–10
alternative thinking, 43–44, 47, 51
Amabile, Teresa, 42
Amazon, 97–98
Anderson, Jeff, 42
anterior cingulate cortex, 45, 64, 78, 80
anthropology, 51–52
Antioco, John, 55
AOL-Time Warner, 55
Apple, ix–x
ASD. *see* autism spectrum disorder
Asperger's syndrome, 7
association, 30
asymmetric dominance, 67–69
attention, 30, 59–60, 69, 76
attention-deficit/hyperactivity
    disorder (ADHD), 41, 51, 82, 98
audiences, 30, 39
autism spectrum disorder (ASD), 82,
    98–99

Barnett, Sam, 32–33
Baron-Cohen, Simon, 7
baseball, 21–23, 85
BCIs. *see* brain computer interfaces
behavior, viii, 7, 11–12, 17–18, 25
    brains and, xi–xii, 94–95
    of connections, xiii
    of consumers, 99
    economics and, 95–96
    gazes and, 61–62

predictions and, 80–81
routines, 42–43
social brains and, 69, 102
beliefs, 29
Benioff, Marc, 49
Berger, Jonah, 34–35
bias, 7–8, 10–12, 75–76
Blanco, Gregor, 21
blinking rates, 46–47
Blockbuster, 55
BlueJeans, 5
BMIs. *see* brain-machine interfaces
Bochy, Bruce, 21–22
Bock, Laszlo, 73–74
body language, 32
BP. *see* British Petroleum
brain computer interfaces (BCIs), 88
Brain Research through Advancing
    Innovative Neurotechnologies
    Initiative, 96–97
brain-machine interfaces (BMIs), 88
brains, 1–6, 10–15, 20–21, 25,
    101–103. *see also* neuroscience;
    social brains
    aging and, 73
    anterior cingulate cortex, 45, 64,
        78, 80
    behavior and, xi–xii, 94–95
    creativity in, 42–44, 51–53
    during decision-making, 69,
        81–82
    dopamine, 47, 74–75
    dorsomedial prefrontal cortex,
        81–82
    emotions and, 91
    exercise for, 53

About the Author

Michael Platt is a scientist known for asking some of the most challenging questions in 21st-century neuroscience—and conceiving innovative ways to find the answers. Principle questions focus on the biological mechanisms that underlie decision-making and social interaction, the grasp of which has broad-scale implications for improving health, welfare, and business in societies worldwide. Broad expertise in anthropology, psychology, economics, evolutionary biology, ethology, and marketing, in addition to collaborations with colleagues in these fields, has enabled him to reach ever-deeper levels of understanding about the neural bases of decision-making and cognition. Current interests focus on applying insights and technology from brain science to business, particularly questions in marketing, management, finance, and innovation.

As a Penn Integrates Knowledge professor, he has appointments in the Department of Neuroscience in the Perelman School of Medicine, the Department of Psychology in the School of Arts and Sciences, and the Department of Marketing in the Wharton School.

Michael received his BA at Yale and his PhD at Penn, both in anthropology, and did a postdoctoral fellowship in neuroscience at NYU. His work has been supported by the National Institutes of Health, the Klingenstein Foundation, the McDonnell Foundation, the EJLB Foundation, the Simons Foundation, the Kaufman Foundation, and the Department of Defense, among others. He won a

MERIT award from the National Institute of Mental Health and was an Alfred P. Sloan Foundation fellow. Michael has authored over 140 peer-reviewed papers and over 60 review and opinion papers, and his work has been cited over 15,800 times.

A revered instructor, Michael won the Master Teacher/Clinician Award from the Duke University School of Medicine and the Teaching Commitment and Curricular Innovation Award from the Wharton School. He is the former director of the Duke Institute for Brain Sciences and the Center for Cognitive Neuroscience at Duke, and the founding codirector of the Duke Center for Neuroeconomic Studies. Michael's work has been featured in the *New York Times, Washington Post, Wall Street Journal, Newsweek, The Guardian,* and *National Geographic,* as well as on ABC's *Good Morning America,* NPR, CBC, BBC, MTV, and HBO Vice. He currently serves on the scientific advisory boards of several companies, served on the World Economic Forum Global Future Council on Brain Science, consulted on the film *The Fountain* by Darren Aronofsky, and is cofounder of Cogwear Technologies, a brain science start-up.

About Wharton School Press

Wharton School Press, the book publishing arm of the Wharton School of the University of Pennsylvania, was established to inspire bold, insightful thinking within the global business community.

Wharton School Press publishes a select list of award-winning, best-selling, and thought-leading books that offer trusted business knowledge to help leaders at all levels meet the challenges of today and the opportunities of tomorrow. Led by a spirit of innovation and experimentation, Wharton School Press leverages groundbreaking digital technologies and has pioneered a fast-reading business book format that fits readers' busy lives, allowing them to swiftly emerge with the tools and information needed to make an impact. Wharton School Press books offer guidance and inspiration on a variety of topics, including leadership, management, strategy, innovation, entrepreneurship, finance, marketing, social impact, public policy, and more.

Wharton School Press also operates an online bookstore featuring a curated selection of influential books by Wharton School faculty and Press authors published by a wide range of leading publishers.

To find books that will inspire and empower you to increase your impact and expand your personal and professional horizons, visit *wsp.wharton.upenn.edu.*

Wharton
UNIVERSITY *of* PENNSYLVANIA

About the Wharton School

Founded in 1881 as the world's first collegiate business school, the Wharton School of the University of Pennsylvania is shaping the future of business by incubating ideas, driving insights, and creating leaders who change the world. With a faculty of more than 235 renowned professors, Wharton has 5,000 undergraduate, MBA, executive MBA, and doctoral students. Each year 13,000 professionals from around the world advance their careers through Wharton Executive Education's individual, company-customized, and online programs. More than 99,000 Wharton alumni form a powerful global network of leaders who transform business every day.

www.wharton.upenn.edu